Living in Christ

Living in Christ

Overcoming Challenges and Finding Purpose

HENRIQUE PESCH

WIPF & STOCK · Eugene, Oregon

LIVING IN CHRIST
Overcoming Challenges and Finding Purpose

Copyright © 2025 Henrique Pesch. All rights reserved. Except for brief quotations in critical publications or reviews, no part of this book may be reproduced in any manner without prior written permission from the publisher. Write: Permissions, Wipf and Stock Publishers, 199 W. 8th Ave., Suite 3, Eugene, OR 97401.

Wipf & Stock
An Imprint of Wipf and Stock Publishers
199 W. 8th Ave., Suite 3
Eugene, OR 97401

www.wipfandstock.com

PAPERBACK ISBN: 979-8-3852-6057-7
HARDCOVER ISBN: 979-8-3852-6058-4
EBOOK ISBN: 979-8-3852-6059-1

VERSION NUMBER 10/23/25

Unless otherwise indicated, all Scripture quotations taken from The Holy Bible, New International Version®, NIV®. Copyright © 1973, 1978, 1984, 2011 by Biblica, Inc. Used with permission of Zondervan. All rights reserved worldwide. www.zondervan.com. Scripture quotations marked (NASB) taken from the New American Standard Bible. Copyright 1999–2024 © The Lockman Foundation. All Rights Reserved. Scripture quotations marked (NKJV) taken from the New King James Version®. Copyright © 1982 by Thomas Nelson. Used by permission. All rights reserved. Scripture quotations marked (ESV) are from The ESV® Bible (The Holy Bible, English Standard Version®), © 2001 by Crossway, a publishing ministry of Good News Publishers. Used by permission. All rights reserved. Scripture marked (NRV) taken from La Biblia Nueva Reina-Valera 2000. © Emanuel Bible Society, 2020. All rights reserved.

To all my brothers and sisters
at Reach Assembly of God in Hyannis, USA,
who have been a source of love, fellowship,
and growth for my life and my family.

Contents

Acknowledgments | ix
Introduction | xi

1. Priorities | 1
2. Living Christian Fellowship | 9
3. Money, "My Precious" | 16
4. My Marriage, My Blessing | 26
5. Triumphing over Sin | 34
6. What Is My Calling? | 45
7. Controlling Social Media | 55
8. Taking Care of My Body | 65
9. My Children, My Inheritance | 74
10. Finding Satisfaction in My Work | 84
11. Waiting on the Lord | 90
12. Living the Word | 101

Bibliography | 115

Acknowledgments

To the Lord God for the breath of life and his wonderful grace. For saving me through the precious blood of Jesus. To him be all honor, glory, and praise.

To my beloved wife Francieli, always by my side, encouraging me and contributing so much to this book through her life and example. To my children, Daniel and Heloisa, who are my source of joy. How wonderful it is to see them growing in the grace and knowledge of Jesus.

To my pastor, Dennis Marcelino da Silva, who has been a blessing in my life and family. His life has been an example for our entire church.

To my church, Reach Assembly of God in Hyannis, Massachusetts, and its leadership. It is a great privilege to be part of a dynamic church, guided by the Holy Spirit, that seeks to exalt the name of Jesus above all names.

To Wipf and Stock Publishers who helped make this project a reality.

Introduction

THE INTENT OF THIS book is to make us reflect on our life in Christ and how to overcome some challenges that arise so that we can live fully and with purpose. Someone once said that salvation is free, but becoming a disciple of Christ will cost us everything we have. Yes, but this statement should not be seen as an unbearable burden that we must carry with our own strength throughout life. Jesus himself said that his burden is light, and that is the burden he wants us to carry (Matt 11:29–30). However, he also said that if we want to follow him, we must deny ourselves, take up our cross, and follow him (Luke 9:23).

The truth is, he would not have said this if it were not possible. He wants us to live an abundant life. That is why he came—not only to save us but also so that we could live fully in his presence (John 10:10). This does not mean we will have a life free of suffering, defeats, or struggles, but rather a life of growth and continuous transformation in his image. God sent the Holy Spirit to help us in this process. And we have our guide for faith and conduct—the word of God.

The abundant and purposeful life that Jesus speaks of is not just about the salvation of our souls; he desires that every sphere of our lives be influenced and transformed by our faith in him. Our perspective—the way we see the world and everything we have—must be shaped by the word.

Introduction

After John the Baptist preached a hard message about preparing the way and producing fruits of repentance in light of the coming of the Lamb of God, people asked him what they should do. He did not merely tell them to have fellowship with the Lord and be content with that. Their fruits of repentance had to permeate all areas of their lives. That is why he exhorted them to share their clothing and food with those in need—to love others in a practical way. He instructed them on how to handle money, how to behave at work, and how to be satisfied with what they had. When we superficially analyze John the Baptist, we might see him as someone detached from daily life, but his exhortations show us that true Christianity must infiltrate every aspect of our daily living in this world (Luke 3:4–14).

Thus, these practical topics have been selected to help us reflect on our Christian journey and its challenges. I start with our priorities, which lay the foundation for our structure, and cover themes such as family, money, temptation, and even contemporary issues like social media. Additionally, I highlight areas that can strengthen our faith and trust, such as waiting on the Lord and the necessity of living the word. My hope is that through this book, you will desire and seek to be increasingly transformed by the Lord and his word. May your life, in all its different moments, be completely influenced by your faith and trust in Jesus.

1

Priorities

Examine yourselves to see whether you are in the faith; test yourselves.
—2 Corinthians 13:5

A SHORT STORY FOR us to reflect on: A missionary was in a city, preaching the gospel at night, and it was raining heavily. He was then invited by a wealthy farmer to stay at his house. The farmer took the "poor missionary" to see all his possessions. The missionary remained silent, so the farmer asked what he thought of everything he had. The missionary simply replied, "I just want to know how much you are investing in the kingdom of heaven."

It is very true that we worry and spend a lot of energy trying to be well in all aspects of our lives. We want to be secure in our material and emotional lives, in our relationships with family, friends, colleagues, managers, church brothers, and so on. We strive to achieve and progress in many areas. There is nothing wrong with that. But there are priorities.

A CONSTANT QUESTION

How is my relationship with God? This is a question we should ask ourselves. It is not about how it was a year ago, last Sunday at church, or at an event where we were deeply moved by God's presence. Nor is it about how it will be months or years from now when we think we will have more time for him after overcoming certain challenges. The question is for today: How is my relationship with the Lord today?

It would be pointless to discuss so many important issues that influence us if we do not first address our walk with the Lord. There will not truly be a fulfilling life with purpose that overcomes all challenges if we do not ask this question and assess our relationship with the Father. And when we ask this question sincerely and evaluate our spiritual condition, we can take the first step toward transforming what needs to change in our lives.

THE VANITY OF LIFE

Let's go back to the Bible. Today, many people read so many things but dedicate little to no time to reading the word. We can read a lot, but nothing can replace the Scriptures in our lives. I want to go to the book of Ecclesiastes (2:1–11), which is a very profound text.

Did you know that many secular scholars consider Ecclesiastes one of the highest forms of philosophical writing? But we know that beyond philosophy, this book contains rich spiritual teachings for all of us. The name Ecclesiastes means "preacher" or "one who gathers an assembly" and acts as its spokesman.[1] This man was not just any priest or prophet but a wise man giving counsel.

From the first verse of the book, which says, "The words of the Preacher, the son of David, king in Jerusalem" (1:1 KJV) it is attributed to Solomon, the son of David, who surpassed all in wisdom.

---

1. In Hebrew, the word is *Qōheleth*, meaning "preacher." See Zodhiates and Warren, *Hebrew-Greek*, 774.

Solomon was responsible for building the temple in Jerusalem, a privilege his father, David, did not have. He also built other great structures, such as the royal palace, the palace for the high priest, the palace of the pharaoh's daughter, the House of the Forest of Lebanon, and the Hall of Columns. During his forty-year reign, there was peace in the kingdom, and Israel's borders expanded as never before. His wealth and glory were greater than all the kings before him. He had seven hundred wives and three hundred concubines. He wrote the books of Proverbs, Ecclesiastes, and Song of Solomon. His wisdom was so extraordinary that the queen of Sheba traveled from Africa to Jerusalem to witness his wisdom and wealth. The Bible says that when she saw it all and heard him speak, "she was breathless" (1 Kgs 10:5 NASB). She was astonished, realizing that Solomon's reputation was indeed true.

Yet, despite possessing and accomplishing everything a human being could dream of—wealth, power, glory, wisdom, and women (according to the customs of that time)—his heart drifted away from the one who should have been first. God's law was no longer his priority. This man had everything we often chase after so anxiously, yet in the end he realized the futility of pursuing material things and temporary pleasures for happiness and peace.

WHO WOULDN'T WANT THAT?

Let's be honest—saying that material possessions, glory, and power are bad is often an excuse used by those who don't have them, right? Who doesn't enjoy achieving and acquiring things? We shouldn't be hypocritical and claim that money is evil. Money can indeed bring many benefits and comfort to our lives.

Notice that Jesus never demanded that Nicodemus (John 3) or Zacchaeus (Luke 19:1–9) sell all their possessions when they encountered him. In fact, Jesus spoke a lot about money in the Gospels, often using it in his parables. What the Bible condemns is the love of money. Paul clearly states, "For the love of money is a root of all kinds of evil. Some people, eager for money, have wandered from the faith and pierced themselves with many griefs" (1 Tim 6:10).

Solomon, in his later years, warns us about the dangers of being drawn to the values, riches, and philosophies of this world to the point where they become the sole focus of our energy and lives.

By no means do I intend to write against working hard and striving to acquire things. We should indeed do so. One must study, work, and excel in what they do. There is no magic formula for progressing in life other than this, as it is right before God and men. The point is that all these things, no matter how good and desirable they may be, are temporary and will not ultimately bring full joy.

SETTING PRIORITIES

Solomon realized that everything he had gained—wealth, power, wisdom, and every pleasure—did not bring true fulfillment.

Today, many people dedicate themselves entirely to work, education, travel, entertainment, and other pursuits, believing these things will bring them happiness while neglecting what truly matters. They assume they must first "enjoy life" before committing to God. Others occasionally reflect on their priorities but quickly return to their earthly pursuits and temporary pleasures once the moment of inspiration fades.

A well-known book, *The Tyranny of the Urgent*, conveys a simple but profound message: "Do not let what is urgent take the place of what is important in your life."[2]

Today, the urgent is taking over the lives of many Christians while the important is being set aside. We need to take a step back from the urgent tasks we face daily. Let me ask you a question: What do you consider the "top priority" in your life? This is a very serious question, and you may need some time to reflect on it.

---

2. Hummel, *Tyranny of the Urgent*, 4.

REMEMBER

At the end of book Ecclesiastes, it says: "Remember your Creator" (12:1). The Hebrew verb for "remember" also carries the meaning of "recognize." And recognizing is more than just recalling something or someone. To recognize is to give due value and respect. When I say that I recognize my father, it means that I give him the respect and value he deserves; otherwise, it is just words. Merriam-Webster.com also defines "recognizing" as "to admit as being lord or sovereign."[3]

And see what the text tells us to remember or recognize—our Creator, the one who made us and created all things. The same one that the prophet Isaiah says measured the oceans in the hollow of his hands and the heavens with the span of his hand (Isa 40:12). The same one who made Adam from the dust of the earth and breathed into him the breath of life (Gen 2:7). The one who declares that he owns the silver and the gold (Hag 2:8). The one who, after Job complained about his unjust suffering, asked him where he was when he laid the foundations of the earth and set the boundaries of the sea (Job 38:4).

In other words, we are not just remembering any person or being, as when we recall important people on their birthdays. We are remembering, or recognizing, the one who has all power in heaven and on earth. Solomon is giving us a rational directive to acknowledge what is of the highest priority—our Creator, without whom we can do nothing, and everything becomes mere vanity and chasing after the wind (Eccl 2:11).

IDOLS OF THE HEART

Perhaps you are reading this and thinking, "I go to church regularly. In fact, I have been going to church since I was a child; I practically grew up in the church." However, Jesus met a young man who had been going to church since childhood and who kept all the commandments (Luke 18:18–23). Unfortunately, though,

---

3. Merriam-Webster.com, "Recognize."

this young man was religious, a church member, but he had an idol in his heart—his wealth.

You might conclude, "I don't have riches to idolize, so this doesn't apply to me!" A great mistake—riches are not the only things that can dethrone Jesus from our hearts. Your family can take Jesus' place in your heart; a job that consumes all your energy and motivation; an education degree that you idolize; a hobby that starts taking so much of your time that you don't even realize it; a ministry in the church where you work hard, but in reality, it's more about self-affirmation than a true service of love for God. Notice how many things, not necessarily wealth, can become idols in your life.

And there's no point in using the excuse that you don't have enough time for God. We all have the same amount of time—twenty-four hours a day. It's a matter of priorities. In this season of your life, with all the activities you are involved in, God wants to have first place.

THE MOST IMPORTANT FIRST

One day, Jesus passed through a village called Bethany and stayed at the house of two sisters named Martha and Mary—a well-known story. Martha was busy and worried about organizing things and serving. Meanwhile, her sister Mary was sitting at the Lord's feet, listening to his teachings. Martha, overwhelmed with so much to do, became upset and asked Jesus to tell her sister to help her. Jesus replied,

> "Martha, Martha," the Lord answered, "you are worried and upset about many things, but few things are needed—or indeed only one. Mary has chosen what is better, and it will not be taken away from her." (Luke 10:41–42).

We must agree on one thing—Martha was doing good and even necessary things. Jesus did not rebuke her for what she was doing, but rather for her need to reassess her priorities. Many people, including Christians, find themselves in this situation—anxious and worried about many things. Often, they want to serve without first listening to Jesus!

CHOOSING THE BEST PART

There is one thing that will never end. We will be separated from everything else in this life, but there is one thing that nothing can separate us from—the love of God in Christ Jesus. Paul says,

> For I am convinced that neither death nor life, neither angels nor demons, neither the present nor the future, nor any powers, neither height nor depth, nor anything else in all creation, will be able to separate us from the love of God that is in Christ Jesus our Lord. (Romans 8:38–39).

As the biblical commentator Matthew Henry said, "Christ declared that Mary had chosen the better part. Only one thing is necessary, and that was precisely what she chose—to submit to the direction of the Lord Jesus Christ."[4]

Therefore, choose the best part. That doesn't mean you should abandon everything. Choosing the best part means surrendering completely to the lordship of Christ in your life and not allowing your many occupations make you forget that your priority is your fellowship with God.

Choosing the best part means recognizing that everything I have comes from God—my health, family, friends, job, education, ministry—so I will give due value to the one from whom "every good and perfect gift" comes (Jas 1:17). And although all these things are blessings from God, I will not place them above the Giver of blessings.

Choosing the best part means dedicating part of my daily time to prayer, reading, and meditating on the word as a precious and planned time, rather than something I do on a rush.

We live in an increasingly materialistic and consumeristic society where love is growing cold. Even within our churches, the

---

4. Henry, *Matthew Henry's Commentary*, 840.

love of many has also diminished—that is, love for God and consequently for one another. Do not be swayed by the ways of this world, and do not base your spiritual life on moments of "revival" in churches. Evaluate your spiritual condition daily.

Perhaps you find yourself like Martha, constantly worried about many things and forgetting to be in the presence of the master. By making this evaluation and reassessing your priorities, you will choose the best part.

FOR REFLECTION

1. Examining yourself. What activities are taking up your time that shouldn't?
2. How can you reduce the time spent on them so that your relationship with God becomes a priority?

A PRAYER

Lord, help me, through your Holy Spirit, to place you above everything and everyone in my life. I need more time alone with you. I want to deepen my fellowship with you. I want to have my priorities in the right order, knowing that everything passes but your word remains forever. I need your forgiveness and grace to walk with you and to know you more and more.

2

Living Christian Fellowship

I know nothing more deadly than isolation. No other influence has a more destructive effect on mental and physical health than the separation between people. It has already been discovered that this is one of the central factors in the emergence of illnesses such as depression, paranoia, schizophrenia, and acts like rape, suicide, mass murder, and a wide variety of other disorders.

—Philip Zimbardo

God did not create man to live alone; on the contrary, we were created to live in society. We have already seen that many evils result from isolation. That is why we must practice love for our neighbor through commitment and involvement with one another. There are at least four areas of involvement in which we live with other people.

1. **Involvement with God (the most important).** This relationship offers us salvation by God's grace through faith in Jesus

Christ (Rom 5:1). In the present, it requires a daily walk with Christ by faith (Acts 9:31). We need to surrender and trust our plans to him (Phil 4:6).

2. **Involvement with family members.** Spouse, parents, children, siblings, and relatives, whether Christian or not (our closest circle). How are we engaging with them? We often want to bring the world to Christ, but are we helping those in our own household draw closer to him? (Gen 12:3).

3. **Involvement with non-Christians.** Unfortunately, they make up the majority of people in the world. We work, go to school, and live near them. If we do not engage with them, how will we bring them to Christ? To what extent should we get involved? (Matt 5:13–16).

4. **Involvement with other Christians.** Pastor and author Charles Swindoll states,

> These people are usually chosen from among those who attend our church. The number increases as we build relationships with others. Some can even name hundreds of Christian friends with whom they have a relationship. This is an important factor in our journey through life on this planet, which would otherwise be a lonely and discouraging pilgrimage.[1]

Arthur Schopenhauer, the nineteenth-century German philosopher, suggested that we are like a group of porcupines on a cold winter night. The cold forces us to draw close together, forming a compact group to keep warm. But when we get too close, our sharp quills start to prick one another—causing us to move apart. Before long, we feel cold again and huddle together once more, only to prick and hurt each other again. And so we continue in this strange and rhythmic "tribal dance." We cannot deny the fact: we need each other, yet we are always hurting one another.[2]

---

1. Swindoll, *Strengthening Your Grip*, 27.
2. Swindoll, *Strengthening Your Grip*, 28.

HOW CAN WE BREAK THIS "PORCUPINE SYNDROME"?

First, by strengthening our involvement with God and his grace. Second, we urgently need true fellowship. "They devoted themselves to the apostles' teaching and to fellowship, to the breaking of bread and to prayer" (Acts 2:42).

The church had just been born—about three thousand new converts in the streets of Jerusalem. They had little to rely on—no buildings, organization, pastors, choir, Sunday school, norms, or even a complete version of the Bible. What did they do? They remained steadfast in the following:

- **The apostles' teaching** (Prov 15:33)
- **Prayer** (1 Thess 5:17)
- **Breaking of bread** (Gal 6:2)
- **Fellowship** (Acts 2:43–45)

These Christians shared laughter and tears, burdens and joys. "The love of Christ glowing in the hearts of these people called forth also a love for their fellow-disciples, an unity of spirit, [and] a joy in fellowship."[3]

CHARACTERISTICS OF INVOLVEMENT

The apostle Paul gives us important instructions in 1 Corinthians:

> So that there should be no division in the body, but that its parts should have equal concern for each other. If one part suffers, every part suffers with it; if one part is honored, every part rejoices with it. Now you are the body of Christ, and each one of you is a part of it. (12:25–27)

We can list some of these characteristics as the following: cooperation, vulnerability, and responsibility.

---

3. Hurlbut, *Hurlbut's Story of the Christian Church*, 24.

1. Cooperation

In this passage, Paul describes a body with many members, all equally important. He emphasizes the care we must have for each other, ensuring there is no division in the body. Instead, we should work together. Cooperation is *a joint effort for a shared purpose and goal. It is about providing support for a common cause—collaboration and solidarity.*

As members of the body of Christ, we must have a common objective. And what is the common goal of Christ's body? The glory of God through the edification of the whole body. When all members, whether prominent or unnoticed, cooperate, the entire body is built up, and God is glorified. This makes me aware of my responsibility for my brother's well-being. I must intentionally cooperate with him—not just in any way, but with care and love for his benefit.

This stands in contrast to the "selfie" generation that focuses on personal benefit. Think about the Good Samaritan, what advantage did he gain from helping the wounded man? Apparently, none. But he was moved by compassion and wanted the good of his neighbor (Luke 10:25-37). How much more should we act for our fellow believers, considering others more important than ourselves (Phil 2:3).

2. Vulnerability

Verse 26 of 1 Corinthians states, "If one part suffers, every part suffers with it; if one part is honored, every part rejoices with it."

Another characteristic of involvement is vulnerability. The words from the verse above are filled with personal emotion. Those who engage with others make themselves vulnerable to suffering and joy. The problem is that many believers do not want to get involved to the point of suffering for others. However, true involvement means genuinely sharing in another's suffering, making oneself vulnerable. However, it also means sharing in another's honor, without envy, but with true joy.

Christian counselor Larry Crabb states,

> It is a sin of self-protection to offer a mild word to another's suffering when motivated by fear of discomfort. This sin occurs when fear of suffering affects our love for others. When our need for self-protection hinders us from approaching others for their well-being, we violate the law of love.[4]

Consider the story in Mark 14:3. Mary brought a jar of pure nard, broke it, and poured it over Jesus. According to John 12:3, the fragrance filled the entire house. A tremendous story. Similarly, when we enter church on Sunday, we often remain closed within ourselves, exchanging only polite words. But to experience true fellowship, we must be willing to break the jar. It is risky, but necessary. Only through self-denial can we experience the unity God desires, leading to growth, healing, and mutual support.[5]

3. Responsibility

People are becoming increasingly isolated, selfish, and often seeking anonymity. The Polish sociologist Zygmunt Bauman describes modern times as a "liquid society." He explains that this society does not think in the long term, cannot sustain its projects, and no longer has lasting goals. Everything is governed by the capitalist market, where new demands arise almost daily, leading to a loss of the ability to make things last and to uphold principles that regulate the family. This results in a disorderly life.

In this same context, Bauman, in his work *Liquid Love*, discusses precisely the lack of permanence in relationships, where people are treated as disposable, as if relationships slip through our fingers like water. There is no longer the desire or willingness to cultivate healthy relationships; instead, when the first problem arises, it becomes easier to simply "disconnect" or "unfollow."[6]

---

4. Crabb, *Inside Out*, 132.
5. Ortlund, *Up with Worship*, 23.
6. Bauman, *Liquid Love*, 31.

Even in our churches, if we are not careful, we may find ourselves merely attending services without truly engaging. But it should not be this way. Paul says, "Now you are the body of Christ, and each one of you is a part of it" (1 Cor 12:27). We are individuals, but we are also responsible for one another. In an indifferent world, it is reassuring to know that we are part of this great family, the body of Christ on earth. In fact, it is the largest family that exists, because wherever you go in this world, if there is a born-again Christian, the feeling is one of fellowship, belonging, and care.

This week, I heard a brief yet powerful testimony from a sister in our community that perfectly relates to this topic. She shared that she had been going through difficult days, feeling as if no one really cared about what she was experiencing. However, to her surprise, on a normal Monday morning, she received an email from my wife. In it, my wife simply and sincerely expressed that she was praying for her. These words served as a reminder to this sister that she was not alone or forgotten, but that the body of Christ remembered her and was interceding for her.

Our responsibility toward our brothers and sisters is very serious. God once asked Cain about his brother, and the same question applies to us. We are indeed called to be our brothers' keepers. In times of conflict, we must value relationships above the need to be right. Seeking deeper personal involvement with others should not be seen as just a hobby for when we have extra time—it is essential for the survival of the church.[7]

FOR REFLECTION

1. What have been the greatest blessings of fellowship in your life?
2. Besides what you already do, how could you be an even greater blessing to your fellow believers?

---

7. Swindoll, *Strengthening Your Grip*, 37.

A PRAYER

Lord, I thank you for my brothers and sisters. They are a source of strength and comfort in my walk with you. Help me to see and value their qualities and virtues. Use me with love, grace, and wisdom so that we may support one another. Amen.

3

Money, "My Precious"

It doesn't take a lot of money for it to become "my precious," as the creature Gollum called the fatal ring in J. R. R. Tolkien's epic *The Lord of the Rings*.

Indeed, money conveys a sense of pleasure, power, and satisfaction. I remember my first job and my first paycheck. I was only thirteen years old and had just moved to the United States with my family. The priority was my education, but I also worked on weekends and full-time during summer vacation. My first job was at a zoo—yes, I worked at a zoo! I fed the animals, cleaned the cages and the farm animal yard, did gardening, and other tasks.

I remember my fascination when I received my first paycheck. I wasn't quite sure what to do with it, but my joy at that moment was immense. I think this is the same feeling many people experience when they receive their first salary. The problem is that, over time, we realize that those initial paychecks, small but satisfying, are no longer enough to cover all the expenses that increase as life progresses. If you are not from a wealthy family, you quickly notice the need to earn more money to buy things and achieve financial stability.

The truth is that money has enormous importance in our lives. We depend on it for *everything*. However, because the world has inverted values—since "the whole world is under the control of the evil one" (1 John 5:19)—money has reached the status of being the "source of happiness," the thing that will fulfill all our needs.

I once read a devotional where the writer was driving on a highway in Houston, Texas, when he saw a billboard in large letters announcing, "THE GOOD LIFE!" He couldn't wait to get closer and read the smaller print, which explained that "the good life" meant buying a lakefront house starting at one million dollars. This is just one example of how the world has sold the idea that all happiness comes through money and what you can do with it. Just turn on the TV or go online, and you'll see smiling people carrying shopping bags, happily driving their new cars, or "finding" the true joy of life on a Caribbean cruise. And, honestly, these things are really nice, aren't they? No rational person would say they are bad in themselves! Not at all. One of my personal desires is to go on a cruise and see the beautiful places this world has to offer. But that's not the point. The real question is this: Where does our true source of joy come from? And how do we handle money correctly?

RELEVANCE IN THE BIBLE

Money is a serious matter. Howard Dayton, founder of Crown Ministries, a financial training ministry, found about 500 Bible verses on prayer but 2,350 on how to handle money and material possessions. Many of Jesus' parables speak about money.

So, you might be wondering why the Bible talks so much about money. Why did Jesus speak so much about money? Obviously, Jesus didn't come in pursuit of money; he came for your heart and mine. But he knew that we would seek wealth and material possessions, and the importance we would place on money. That's why Jesus said, "Where your treasure is, there your heart will be also" (Luke 12:34). The heart always follows the treasure. If there is something we value and consider important, no matter what it is, our heart will pursue it.

Money is not inherently evil, nor does the Bible say that those who have money are wicked. Let's once and for all bury the old idea that "God loves the poor and hates the rich." Nowhere in the Bible does God condemn the rich for being rich. He does despise dishonest gain, wealth obtained through wrong motives, and a lack of compassion from the wealthy. But some of the holiest people in the Bible, by today's standard, were prosperous individuals: Job, Abraham, Jacob, Joseph, David, Solomon, Josiah, Barnabas, Philemon, and Lydia, to name a few.

We can see that both the wealthy and those who lack material abundance face similar struggles: envy and the greed to have more.

WHAT DID JESUS SAY ABOUT MONEY?

Among the various parables in which Jesus talked about money, I particularly like the one found in Matt 20:1–16. Some Bibles call it the "Parable of the Workers in the Vineyard," while others title it the "Parable of the Dissatisfied Workers." Regardless of the title, this parable illustrates a work custom from Jesus' time and teaches us valuable lessons about how our hearts handle money.

To summarize, the owner of a vineyard went to the marketplace at six a.m. to hire workers (similar to today's day laborers) for a full day's work. After agreeing on the wage, they went to work. The owner later realized he needed more workers, so he returned to the marketplace at nine a.m., noon, three p.m., and five p.m.

At the end of the workday, at six p.m., the vineyard owner instructed his supervisor to pay the workers, starting with those who arrived last. These latecomers were amazed to receive a full day's wage despite working only a few hours. Seeing this, those who had worked since early morning assumed they would receive more. However, they were shocked to receive the same amount (one denarius, a day's wage). They then complained to the vineyard owner: "These men who were hired last worked only one hour, and you have made them equal to us who have borne the burden of the work and the heat of the day" (v. 12 NASB). The owner's response was clear: He told them their payment was fair because it was exactly what was agreed upon and that he had the right to do what he wanted with his own money.

This parable teaches at least two important lessons: the danger of a competitive spirit and the danger of a complaining spirit.

1. The Danger of a Competitive Spirit

When the workers who had toiled for twelve hours saw the wages of those who worked only one hour, they expected to receive more. But when their eyes focused solely on what others had, they lost the ability to appreciate and enjoy their own earnings.

Comparison can be a terrible thing. As human beings, we have a tendency to compare everything—our appearances, clothes, cars, houses, and, inevitably, our salaries. Comparison becomes fertile ground for envy, which has no place in a believer's life. The Bible tells us that Saul rejoiced over his victory against the Philistines, but when he heard that David was praised more than him, his heart hardened, and he "kept a close eye on David" (1 Sam 18:9).

This parable shows us that when we fix our eyes only on what others have, we lose the joy of what we ourselves have. There is nothing worse in a Christian's life than a spirit of comparison and competition. Many people strive to own things just to show off to their friends and family who doubted their success. Others seek possessions solely for status.

The disciples of Jesus, even while walking with him and listening to his teachings, at a certain moment were also tempted by the desire for competition among themselves. In Mark 10:35–45, we are told that the brothers James and John came to Jesus and asked him to seat one of them at his right and the other at his left in his glory. The other ten were furious at the audacity of the two brothers. After some discussion, Jesus taught them that our rulers have authority over us because they exercise power, but in the kingdom of God, it is different. Whoever wants to be great must be the first to serve, for he himself came to serve and not to be served. In other words, in the kingdom of God, there is no room for competitiveness, but rather for considering others as superior to ourselves (Phil 2:3).

2. The Danger of a Complaining Spirit

> When they received it, they began to grumble against the landowner. (Matt 20:11)

The Lord revealed that such complaints are an attack on his goodness and generosity. He also exposed the evil feelings in the hearts of those workers—just as in our own hearts—by saying, in other words, "Are you envious because I am generous?" (v. 15).

Who do we think we are when we complain about the way God acts? It was precisely the murmuring of God's people in the wilderness that stirred his wrath (Num 14). Complaining is an infectious social disease that robs us of joy and contentment in what God provides. Those who only focus on what they lack do not understand the miracle of God's grace and generosity.

This lesson from Jesus teaches us, not only to refrain from complaining about our financial circumstances (which does not mean we cannot pray and believe that God will bless our financial lives if we trust him and do our part) but also in all aspects of life. When the owner of the vineyard asked if he could not do what he wished with what was his, we can apply this to the Lord's work in our lives! Can he not do as he pleases to guide us in his purposes? Can he not use people as he wishes? As the owner of all things, can he not do whatever he wants with them? Of course he can! Therefore, my brother or sister, do not murmur, whether about your salary, your current situation, or certain circumstances in your life. God is in control of everything and can bless you and make you prosper. However, be content with what you have and be faithful in the little so that one day you may receive much.

HONOR THE LORD

A Sunday school magazine published by CPAD a few years ago was titled *God's Wisdom for a Victorious Life: The Relevance of Proverbs and Ecclesiastes* (*Sabedoria de Deus para uma vida vitoriosa: A atualidade de Provérbios e Eclesiastes*). In Lesson 3, Pastor José Gonçalves discussed prosperity in light of the book of Proverbs, using verses such as "Honor the Lord with your wealth, with the firstfruits of all your crops; then your barns will be filled to overflowing, and your vats will brim over with new wine." (Prov 3:9–10).

According to the author, this text clearly teaches that if we want the Lord's blessing on our finances, we need to honor him with our possessions. Such an attitude, according to the wise man, will cause our "barns" to be abundantly filled and our "vats" to overflow. The barn and the vat are metaphors representing a financially abundant life. Honoring the Lord with our possessions means giving our tithes and making voluntary offerings with joy (2 Cor 9:7).[1]

Being a tither is the foundation of a blessed financial life. Returning a portion of our income to him out of obedience, faith, and love protects us from the devourer and attracts God's blessings. You may know people who earn well, but because they are not faithful in tithing and offerings, they constantly struggle financially. Meanwhile, others who earn less, but are faithful, manage their finances more wisely. Maybe this has happened to you—when you realized that things only got worse when you failed to give back to the Lord what belongs to him.

The prophet Malachi uses a strong expression: "Will a mere mortal rob God? Yet you rob me. But you ask, 'How are we robbing you?' In tithes and offerings" (3:8). This verse alone should be enough for us never to neglect giving our tithes and offerings in the house of the Lord. However, some argue, "I earn so little, and 10 percent less will make it hard to pay my bills!" But let me tell you, God's mathematics does not work like ours. He does not

---

1. See Gonçalves, *Sabedoria de Deus*.

need more to bless you. Jesus needed only a young boy's obedience and generosity with five loaves and two fish to multiply and feed a multitude (Matt 14:13-21). With just a little flour and oil, he blessed a poor widow for her willingness to bless a man of God (1 Kgs 17:7-15).

If you have not been a tither and an offering giver until now, or if you have struggled in this area, I challenge you to start today. Forget the past, begin now, and you will surely see God multiplying financial blessings in your life.

BEWARE OF GREED

Another parable of Jesus about money that teaches us a great lesson is found in Luke 12:13-21. This passage forces us to reflect on ourselves.

Jesus was speaking to the crowd when a man brought up a family dispute. It seems he was the younger of two brothers, and the older brother refused to share the inheritance. Since it was common to bring disputes to a rabbi, this man expressed his frustration to Jesus: "Teacher, tell my brother to divide the inheritance with me" (v. 13).

Interestingly, the man did not ask Jesus to judge the situation, but to side with him for financial gain. He wanted to use Jesus to fulfill his financial desires. However, Jesus refused to take a position because that was not his mission. Even today, many seek Jesus only as a means to achieve financial success. Then, Jesus turned to the crowd and warned them: "Watch out! Be on guard against all kinds of greed; life does not consist in the abundance of possessions" (v. 15).

Jesus was not merely talking about a small sin but a serious one—although subtle. Many sins are obvious, and we Christians tend to condemn them harshly. However, we rarely see greed or covetousness as a horrible sin. Yet Jesus warned against it strongly. Greed is simply an insatiable desire for more. This does not mean that ambition and growth are necessarily sinful. God blesses those who are faithful, diligent, and generous. The sin here is the opposition to contentment that comes with true godliness (1 Tim 6:6).

The billionaire John D. Rockefeller was once asked how much money was enough. He replied, "Just one dollar more." The sin of greed is insatiable.

A MATTER OF ATTITUDE

Now, we make a mistake if we see greed only as a matter of desire and not of attitude. A poor person can be covetous, and a rich person can avoid greed. But the danger of possessions is that they awaken the desire to have more. And covetousness is characterized in the Bible as idolatry (Col 3:5). However, Jesus did not settle for giving an abstract warning, so in this passage, he tells a parable about the foolish rich man (vv. 16–21).[2]

This man had acquired wealth, which allowed him to own land that produced a great harvest. Then, "He thought to himself, 'What shall I do? I have no place to store my crops.' Then he said, 'This is what I'll do. I will tear down my barns and build bigger ones, and there I will store my surplus grain. And I'll say to myself, "You have plenty of grain laid up for many years. Take life easy; eat, drink and be merry."' But God said to him, 'You fool! This very night your life will be demanded from you. Then who will get what you have prepared for yourself?'" (vv. 17–20).

Notice that there seems to be no criticism of the fact that the man was rich or how he gained his wealth. Once again, it is not a sin to be rich or have a lot of money. The crucial point was not his actions, but his presumption. We can summarize this man's mindset with various phrases that characterize such people: *Success with possessions proves that I am truly a successful person. If I don't do something for myself, who will? The bigger my barn (house, car, possibility to travel), the better my life will be. Money gives me security.*

But suddenly, everything changed! God pronounced his judgment. And here we highlight a few things:

---

2. Inrig, *Cultivating*, 21.

1. **He was a fool, not a success.** It is almost certain that, in the eyes of the community, he was an envied man. But in God's eyes, he was a fool to be pitied. Biblically, foolishness is not a description of mental capacity, but of spiritual discernment. In the books of Psalms and Proverbs, a fool is a person who makes decisions as if God does not exist.

2. **He had no control over anything.** The rich man thought he was in control of his life because of his wealth. But God said, "This very night your life will be demanded from you" (v. 20). The word "demanded" in the original language was a commercial term for a loan. Here, he discovered a truth that everyone will learn sooner or later—God is the owner of life, and he is simply lending it to us. At any moment, he can take it back.

3. **He was a poor man, not a rich one.** I once heard someone say that there are people so poor that the only thing they have is money. This man realized that he had worked so hard for so little. He had invested his entire life in what is temporary rather than in what is eternal. "This was a man who left everything behind—the barns he had built, the people he had controlled, the prestige he had gained. Death stripped him completely and revealed who he truly was: a man who 'stores up things for himself but is not rich toward God.'"[3]

Unfortunately, many people are in this condition today. The crucial question in life is not the quantity of our possessions but where they are located. This man's treasures were on earth. He built his life, invested his time and resources in what does not last. As disciples of Christ, we must be rich toward God. No one wants to be called a fool by God. We need to examine our hearts and close the gaps that allow the illusion of power and control that money brings. Our life is in God, and our trust is in him. Everything we have belongs to him.

---

3. Inrig, *Cultivating*, 9.

FOR REFLECTION

1. How have you been handling money in your life?
2. What have you learned in this chapter about finances?

A PRAYER

Lord, everything I have comes from you—my health to work, my provision. Help me manage the money I earn wisely, always honoring you with my resources. May I have control over money and may it not have control over me. Though it is important in my life, may money never take hold of my heart, for my heart belongs to you.

4

My Marriage, My Blessing

The state of marriage is that which requires more virtue and constancy than any other. It is a perpetual exercise of mortification . . . a holy life.
—Francis de Sales

God designed marriage to be a blessing in a person's life. This does not mean it will always be a smooth journey. Every married person reading this book can attest to that. However, marriage is the human relationship that transforms a person like no other.

There was a medieval belief that Christian spirituality was almost synonymous with celibacy, where individuals devoted themselves to long periods of prayer and meditation. The church in the Middle Ages valued and encouraged this style of life, believing that one could get closer to God without marrying (even though the "first pope"—Peter, according to Catholic tradition—was married).

Although the apostle Paul recommended remaining single to have the freedom to focus solely on the things of God (1 Cor 7), he did not forbid marriage. Both states are valid if one is dedicated to the Lord. In fact, I believe marriage is an excellent platform for being transformed into Christ's likeness in a unique way.

SEEKING GOD THROUGH MARRIAGE

The idea of seeking God through marriage has rarely been considered. Instead, people have thought they should seek God despite marriage. Someone once asked a pastor about marriage, and he responded,

> If you want to remain single to serve Jesus, do so. Marriage does take a lot of time and energy, but if you want to become more like Jesus, I can't think of anything better than getting married. Marriage forces you to confront character issues that you would not otherwise face.[1]

According to this pastor, he realized early in his marriage that he could deepen his pursuit of God through marriage.

Transformation in marriage is a twenty-four seven commitment, shaping us into Christ's character. Instead of waking up at three a.m. for prayer in a monastery, the question becomes, "Who will get up to change the baby's diaper?" or "Who will comfort a teenager after a tough day at school?" For couples without children, it could be, "Who will take responsibility for this household task?" Marriage demands an entirely new and selfless life.

Any situation that confronts our selfishness holds great spiritual value. As pastor Gary Thomas said, he slowly began to understand that the primary purpose of marriage is not so much "happiness" as it is "holiness."[2] This does not mean the two are mutually exclusive (in fact, I believe holiness leads to happiness, and this happens in marriage), but viewing marriage through the lens of holiness gives us a different perspective.

---

1. Thomas, *Sacred Marriage*, 23.
2. Thomas, *Sacred Marriage*, 11–13.

THE REDEEMING POWER OF MARRIAGE

It is obvious that this does not mean marriage has the same redeeming power as Christ's atoning sacrifice. However, marriage does possess some redeeming qualities. One of the clearest is found in 1 Cor 7:2—"But since sexual immorality is occurring, each man should have sexual relations with his own wife, and each woman with her own husband." Marriage is the only state permitted by God for sexual relations. Therefore, marriage is a means by which God redeems us sexually.

Beyond redeeming us from the immorality prevalent in our world and our fallen nature, marriage has the power to redeem other areas of our character. It provides the ideal environment for personal transformation, confronting selfishness, anger, impatience, and misunderstanding, among other flaws.

Only by facing my own failures can I overcome them and become a better person through God's grace and the power of the Holy Spirit. Marriage continually places someone before me to love, through a lifelong covenant, making it a powerful instrument for change.

MY MARRIAGE DOES NOT FULFILL EVERYTHING

I cannot expect my wife Francieli to make me happy in the ultimate sense. That fulfillment can only be found in God, in his plan of salvation, in his purpose for my life, and in his promise of eternal presence with him. I can say that I have found great fulfillment in my marriage, seeing it as a lifelong commitment. However, we must remember that marriage is temporary in light of eternity. My relationship with God and my wife's relationship with God will outlast our marriage. Because of this, we seek God together, recognizing that only he gives true meaning to our lives.

We can and should make our daily life together more enjoyable, improve intimacy, and strive to please one another (1 Cor 7:33). But our greatest need is to draw closer to the Lord, who knows us completely. If this relationship is growing, we will place fewer demands on each other, not expecting marriage to be the ultimate source of fulfillment. If our deepest need is not satisfied, we will never feel "fulfilled," no matter how many of our "desires" are met. This is why our fulfillment in God is the foundation of a happy life, where marriage plays a significant role but expecting more from it than it can provide will ultimately harm it.[3]

Many marital dissatisfactions stem from expecting too much from marriage. Despite being a wonderful institution of God's love, he did not create it to compete with him, but to lead us to him.

EXPRESSING GOD IN MARRIAGE

One way we express God in marriage is through the miracle of creation. The first thing we learn about God in Genesis is that he is the Creator of all things (Gen 1:1). The last image of God in the New Testament shows him creating new heavens and a new earth (Rev 21:5). When a couple brings a child into the world, they express the wonder of God's creative power.

Beyond creation, we express God in marriage through the symbolic relationship between Christ (the bridegroom) and his bride (the church). The prophet Isaiah highlights how God delights in his people: "As a bridegroom rejoices over his bride, so will your God rejoice over you" (Isa 62:5). Jesus frequently referred to himself as the bridegroom (Matt 9:15; John 3:27–30). Paul develops this idea in Eph 5:25–27:

> Husbands, love your wives, just as Christ loved the church and gave himself up for her, to make her holy, cleansing her by the washing with water through the word, and to present her to himself as a radiant church, without stain or wrinkle or any other blemish, but holy and blameless.

John reinforces this in the book of Revelation when he speaks of the "wedding supper of the Lamb" (19:9) where the bride (the church) is ready. Jesus himself said that the kingdom of heaven is

---

3. Thomas, *Sacred Marriage*, 26.

like a "wedding banquet" (Matt 22:1–14). And within the beauty of marriage, we express our faithfulness to the Lord through our faithfulness to one another, which has also been portrayed several times, such as by the prophet Jeremiah (3:8) and Hosea (2:16, 19).

And what can be said about the Song of Solomon, which portrays the divine origin of the joy and dignity of human love in marriage? In an allegorical sense, this book also represents the love between God and Israel and between Christ and the church—a love that is undivided, devoted, and strictly personal, to which no one else has access.

WAITING FOR MY WIFE

Like many young people, I faced uncertainty about whom I would date and marry, made wrong choices, felt emotionally vulnerable, and resisted temptations. However, I also learned to wait on the Lord for this blessing.

Waiting on the Lord does not mean things will fall from the sky or that a prince or princess will arrive on a white horse, singing medieval ballads. You remain attentive, sensitive, building relationships, and making choices. The difference is that anxiety and distress are surrendered to God, allowing you to trust and live in peace.

I remember when I entrusted this area of my life to God, things started to fall into place. Francieli was a friend from church whom I admired. It was not just that she was and still is very beautiful, but her commitment to God stood out.

We began talking more in Sunday school, and I realized that a young woman serious about studying God's word was worth considering. Within a year, we dated, got engaged, and married. The Lord has been faithful and has blessed our union.

AS GOD SEES IT

We need to embrace marriage as God sees it. When we read the Bible, we see that this union is a holy institution of God when two become one flesh (Gen 2:24). It is also a special blessing from the Lord. It was not Adam, but God himself who took the initiative to provide him with a companion. In the same way, God continues to provide, and those who place their trust in him will enjoy the same blessing.

Another fundamental characteristic is that marriage is a firm and indissoluble union for life. In our countries, marriage is confirmed and legalized in a civil registry office and not merely by mutual consent. We can see the biblical example of Rebekah. Jacob Graf states,

> Consider the biblical example of Rebekah in Genesis 24. She gave her consent by saying, "I will go" (verse 58). But it is only nine verses later that we read, "She became his wife" (verse 67). The first verse presents marriage as an agreement between two people; the latter demonstrates the public act in relation to society.[4]

Today, the state only recognizes marriage when it is officially registered. It is not enough to have a ceremony and receive the pastor's blessing without a civil wedding—legally, the person remains single. And as we respect and are subject to the laws of the state, we fulfill them as both citizens and Christians (Rom 13:1–7). Furthermore, the state's recognition of marriage as a family entity provides rights and protection to the couple, such as joint custody of children. A civil marriage is a powerful testimony, as it proves that the couple desires a serious commitment that is recognized by everyone in society.

---

4. Note-se o exemplo bíblico de Rebeca, em Genesis 24. Ela deu o seu consentimento, dizendo: "Irei" (versículo 58). Mas é somente nove versículos mais à frente que nos é dito: "Foi-lhe por mulher" (versículo 67). O primeiro versículo apresenta o casamento como um acordo entre duas pessoas; o último demonstra o ato público em relação à sociedade. Graf, *Falando francamente*, 37.

MARRIAGE: A SHARED LIFE

This may seem somewhat obvious, but it is always good to remember this truth: Marriage was not given only to ensure human offspring (Gen 1:28), but also to establish an intimate fellowship of spirit, soul, and body. That is why marriage requires pure and selfless love, faithfulness, trust, and a sense of responsibility.

It has been said that a single person may fly higher, but a married person flies farther. In marriage, one cannot think only about *my* projects, *my* desires, *my* career—everything must be considered in light of the other person. Even when it is just the couple, and even more so when there are children, one cannot simply wake up one day and think, "Today, I'll wake up, leave early, grab breakfast somewhere, go to work, then hit the gym, and later visit a friend's house." Everything must be done with the family in mind.

In this regard, spouses must understand that both should grow in every possible area. For this to happen, they need to encourage, support, compromise, and face challenges together. On a practical level, for my wife to have her quiet devotional time, I need to take care of the children and manage the household. For me to go out and fulfill my ministry at church, she must do the same. If she wants to develop the talents God has given her—like my wife with her musical gifts—I must be willing to sacrifice some of my own time, which could have been invested in my work, to support her. At times, I thought, *I could be focusing on my activities, but here I am carrying boxes for her events, literally.* However, I soon realized that this "effort" brings incredible blessings when I see her fulfilling what God has placed in her hands for his glory. This is not just *her* victory, it is *ours* because we are a family.

This shared life should not be seen as one person losing so the other can win. When one wins, everyone wins. When one loses, everyone loses. This life together is wonderful when we understand its purpose and intentionally strive to live it fully.

FOR REFLECTION

1. How do you see your marriage today?
2. Based on the topics covered in this chapter, is there any area of your marriage that could improve? How?

A PRAYER

Lord, thank you so much for the spouse you have given me. He/She is a blessing to me. I have a covenant with him/her for my entire life. I want to be the husband/wife that you want me to be. Help me to live out my marriage according to the standards of your word. May we grow together in the grace and knowledge of Jesus and support one another in all areas of our lives. Amen!

5

Triumphing over Sin

If you and sin are friends, you and God are not yet reconciled.
—J. C. Ryle

The reality of sin is an unavoidable part of life. It's important to recognize this truth: Those who have not been born again remain under the power of sin. However, when we experience the new birth, we are set free from sin's dominion—even though its presence still lingers. True freedom from sin's presence will only come when we are eternally with the Lord.

Every believer—young or old—faces the challenge of temptation. From the very beginning, humanity has wrestled with this, as seen when the first couple on Earth gave in to the serpent's lure to eat from the tree of the knowledge of good and evil.

Temptation always appeals to something within us. It promises pleasure and seeks to awaken desires rooted in our old nature—our instincts, wants, and longings. But when we entertain temptation or give in to it, it leads us into sin.

Dietrich Bonhoeffer was one of the great theological thinkers of the twentieth century. He was a Lutheran pastor who was a member of the German anti-Nazi resistance during World War II. He was arrested by the Nazis for helping a group of Jews escape to Switzerland. Condemned for treason, he was executed by hanging in the Flossenbürg concentration camp in 1945. During his imprisonment, Bonhoeffer wrote about various important theological issues. One example is a short passage on the subject of temptation. Read his words:

> In our members there is a slumbering inclination towards desire which is both sudden and fierce. With irresistible power desire seizes mastery over the flesh. All at once, a secret, smouldering fire is kindled. The flesh burns and is in flames. It makes no difference whether it is a sexual desire, an ambition, or vanity, or desire for revenge, or love of fame and power, or greed for money, or, finally, the strange desire for the beauty of the world, of nature. Joy in God is in course of being extinguished in us and we seek all our joy in the creature. At this moment God is quite unreal to us, he loses all reality, and only desire for the creature is real; the only reality is the devil. Satan does not here fill us with hatred for God, but with forgetfulness of God. And now his falsehood is added to this proof of strength. The lust thus aroused envelops the mind and will of man in deepest darkness. The powers of clear discrimination and of decision are taken from us. . . . It is here that everything within me rises up against the Word of God.[1]

What a strong statement! No matter who we are or where we are—we can be tempted to sin.

SO, WHAT IS TEMPTATION?

It is the approach of sin. A person is enticed, drawn to commit an act that definitely displeases God, with the promise of obtaining pleasure or some gratifying reward.

1. Bonhoeffer, *Creation and Temptation*, 116–17.

Therefore, it is not a sin to be tempted, but the sin lies in giving in to temptation. John says: "For everything in the world—the lust of the flesh, the lust of the eyes, and the pride of life—comes not from the Father but from the world" (1 John 2:16).

This is exactly what happened with Adam and Eve in humanity's first temptation:

1. **Lust of the flesh**—the fruit was good for food!
2. **Lust of the eyes**—it was pleasing to the eyes!
3. **Pride of life**—it was desirable for gaining wisdom!

Unfortunately, the first couple gave in to this temptation, bringing the curse of sin upon all humanity. And it is precisely sin, or our iniquities, that separate us from God; as the prophet Isaiah says, "But your iniquities have separated you from your God; your sins have hidden his face from you, so that he will not hear" (Isa 59:2).

Our very sins cause God not to hear us! Sometimes we wonder why God does not listen to us. The answer is clear in this text—our iniquities! We must be extremely careful and constantly alert to reject what seems good to our flesh, eyes, and even understanding, but directly leads us into sin and distances us from the Lord's presence.

THE PROCESS OF THE DEVELOPMENT OF TEMPTATION

> But each person is tempted when they are dragged away by their own evil desire and enticed. Then, after desire has conceived, it gives birth to sin; and sin, when it is full-grown, gives birth to death. (Jas 1:14–15)

Temptation follows a process of development. The apostle James clearly outlines how this happens:

Phase 1—Curiosity. Satan casts the bait. We are tempted by our own desire.

"Each person is tempted . . . by their own evil desire."

Phase 2—Seduction. The person approaches the temptation.

"Each person .. is dragged away ... and enticed."

Phase 3—Conception. The person takes the bait. They give in to temptation.

"Desire has conceived."

Phase 4—Birth. The person is hooked.

"It gives birth to sin."

Phase 5—Death. The final destination is fatal!

"And sin, when it is full-grown, gives birth to death."

THE EXAMPLE OF SAMSON

When discussing temptation, a biblical character that quickly comes to mind is Samson. This man also reminds us of his most remarkable trait—his extraordinary strength, which came from the very Spirit of God.

Samson was one of Israel's judges during a difficult time when the nation was oppressed by the Philistines. Born into a solid home with God-fearing parents, Samson was a miracle, as his mother was barren. But he had been foretold, just as John the Baptist and Jesus himself were, and in addition, the angel revealed God's purpose for the boy's life: "He will take the lead in delivering Israel from the hands of the Philistines" (Judg 13:5b).

This boy had everything at his disposal to become a great leader. His devout parents raised him according to the Lord's precepts; and there was a promise over Samson's life that he would be a great deliverer of Israel. But let me pause here and clarify that promises are only fulfilled in a person's life if they walk in God's will. I have seen people with promises who died prematurely without seeing them fulfilled in their lives. The people of Israel also had the promise of being led into the promised land, but due to disobedience and ungratefulness, only two people from that generation entered it. So, we must be careful when singing "We will not die until God fulfills everything he promised in me" (no matter what I do), but rather understand that he will indeed fulfill everything—if we walk in his path!

Unfortunately, Samson rejected his parents' advice, played with temptation, and ultimately gave in to it. These negative aspects compromised his life. Samson possessed an uncontrolled sensual desire that he did not even attempt to restrain. To illustrate this, the first recorded words of Samson in the book of Judges are "I saw a woman." (Judg 14:2). What a statement! The very first words of the man who was supposed to be Israel's great deliverer and judge at that time were about sensual desire.

ATTITUDES TO AVOID IN SAMSON

By carefully analyzing Samson's story, we can identify four attitudes that were detrimental to his calling. These led him to sin and demonstrated his lack of commitment to God. These attitudes serve as warnings for us to learn from and avoid repeating the same mistakes.

1. Uncontrolled Sensuality

This trait unfortunately followed Samson throughout his life. He focused only on women's appearances and satisfying his carnal desires. This happened when he desired one of the women of Timnah as Samson was only interested in her external beauty. Worse still, his desire was so strong in this regard that he ignored and disregarded his parents' counsel against marrying her, as she was a Philistine—part of Israel's enemy nation.

We cannot deny that men are generally more visually attracted than women, who, in turn, are often drawn to what they hear, kindness, and social behavior. However, as writer and speaker Josh

McDowell states, "We are human beings; we are not animals. God has given us the ability to make moral choices and act accordingly."[2] Samson, however, did not even attempt to control his impulses. In Judg 16, it is recorded that Samson once went to Gaza (a Philistine city), saw a prostitute there, and immediately engaged in relations with her. Later, we read that this Israelite leader once again became attached to a pagan woman, Delilah—the affair that ultimately led to his own destruction.

We need to guide young people, telling them that having sexual impulses is completely normal. However, God has set the right time to fully enjoy them without suffering terrible consequences, and that time is called marriage. They must not be overcome by their impulses, and it is important not to fuel the flesh by watching illicit content, being alone with a boyfriend or girlfriend in compromising situations, or engaging in other behaviors that lead to sin. Married individuals are not immune to temptations in this either. They must avoid and flee from all appearances of evil (1 Thess 5:22).

Paul tells Titus,

> For the grace of God has appeared that offers salvation to all people. It teaches us to say 'No' to ungodliness and worldly passions, and to live self-controlled, upright, and godly lives in this present age. (2:11–12)

We must encourage young people who are waiting. They may feel like the last virgin on the planet, but that is simply not true. There are millions of young people around the world who have chosen to wait until marriage for their first sexual experience. Those who have stood at the altar as virgins can testify that it was worth it. If you have stumbled along the way and lost your virginity, God is good and merciful to forgive your sin and give you the strength to avoid making the same mistake again and to continue waiting until your wedding day. In short, do not give up a blessed future in this area for just a few minutes of pleasure. Wait, control yourself, and trust that God has the best for you.

---

2. McDowell, *Bare Facts*, 137.

For married couples, Solomon's advice in Prov 5:18 is valuable: "May your fountain be blessed, and may you rejoice in the wife of your youth." The relationship between husband and wife should be cultivated, respected, and guided by the word in all areas, including their sexual life. In marriage, sex becomes a source of pleasure and protection for both partners.

2. Poorly Managed Leisure Time

Do you remember the angel's revelation about God's purpose for Samson's life? Yes, it was for him to be a great judge over Israel and to deliver his people from their enemies. However, something led him off the path of his purpose. He chose to spend his time indulging in personal pleasures and amusements that greatly hindered him.

On one occasion, during one of his trips to visit his Philistine girlfriend, Samson killed a lion. On his return, he found a beehive and honey inside the lion's carcass. Without being watchful of his actions, he took some of the honey, thereby breaking one of his Nazirite vows, which forbade him from touching a corpse. Pastor Pablo Artur states,

> The problem is not in feeling or enjoying the results of victory. . . . However, I want to encourage you to value the achievements that God has given you without being deceived. A victory does not mean the elimination of all risks. Celebrate victories, but remain alert to avoid a great disaster after a great triumph. Samson is a clear example of this lack of vigilance. He defeated the lion, but after this significant victory, he plunged into an unprecedented decline—all due to a lack of care, discernment, and watchfulness.[3]

---

3. *O problema não está em sentir ou usufruir dos resultados da vitória. . . . No entanto, quero incentivar você a valorizar as conquistas que Deus proporcionou sem se deixar iludir. Uma vitória não significa a extinção de todos os riscos. Celebre as vitórias, mas mantenha-se em estado de alerta a fim de evitar um grande desastre após uma grande conquista. Sansão é o exemplo claro desta falta de atenção. Ele venceu o leão, mas após esta significativa vitória, mergulhou num processo de decadência sem precedentes, e tudo por falta de cuidado,*

At his wedding feast, Samson began to joke with the Philistines by proposing a riddle to them. Even while dealing with people who sought to destroy his own nation, he misused his time on trivial games that ultimately led to his downfall.

Unfortunately, we see many Christians today who poorly manage their leisure time. In this digital era, many spend endless hours "connected" to trivial and meaningless things. Television, with its countless programs—many of which are inappropriate—also becomes a dangerous distraction.

These are challenges for all of us. We need God's grace and a firm resolve not to be dominated by these "attractions." May Paul's words become a reality in our lives: "'I have the right to do anything,' you say—but not everything is beneficial. 'I have the right to do anything'—but I will not be mastered by anything" (1 Cor 6:12).

3. He Did Not Take His Vows Seriously

Another attitude in Samson's life that we must avoid is failing to take our vows seriously. At some point, he may have recalled his parents' instructions and example, but in his arrogance and self-sufficiency, Samson disregarded his vows to God.

We previously mentioned that he had already broken one of his vows by touching a dead body. Later, because he literally "played with temptation," he ended up revealing his secret to the Philistine woman, Delilah.

If you want to experience victories in your life, you must take your vows and commitments seriously. Naturally, the greatest commitment you have is to live in fellowship with God and his church. However, there are other commitments you make that must also be taken seriously. Let's be more specific. You have a commitment to your family—whether you are married, with your spouse and children, or if you are single, with honoring your family. You also have the commitment to return 10 percent of your

---

discernimento e vigilância. Artur, *Fator Nazireu*, 101–2.

income to the Lord as an act of faith, obedience, and love for God's work. Additionally, you have a commitment to submit to the authorities over you, such as the government—whether you like it or not—and your employer. If you serve in any ministry in the church, you have a commitment before God and the congregation to take it seriously and responsibly.

Unfortunately, I see many brothers and church workers who do not take their commitments to God's work seriously. The fear and reverence for this responsibility have been lost by many. But one thing is certain—those who strive to do their best and take their commitments seriously become targets of God's favor. Dear brother or sister, be someone who faithfully honors your commitments, whatever they may be, and be part of the generation that values and upholds their word.

WHY NOT GIVE IN TO TEMPTATION

Centuries ago, an ordinary Israelite was tempted by his master's wife. She seduced him, saying, "Come to bed with me." (Gen 39:7) But Joseph resisted and replied, "How then could I do such a wicked thing and sin against God?" (Gen 39:9). So Joseph fled the scene. His greatest concern was not his reputation (What if others found out?), but rather, he saw that giving in to temptation would mean sinning against God.

When God's children internalize spiritual values, they remain pure before and during marriage—not out of fear of being caught, nor primarily because of God's punishment, but because they fear the Lord and do not want to be distanced from his presence.

"SUBTLE" SINS

Perhaps you think that the types of sins Samson committed have no hold over you, or that you would not face temptations like Joseph's. However, there are "subtle" sins—if we can call them that—for sin is sin, though the consequences may differ.

One of these sins is *pride*. In the Bible, King Saul serves as a negative example of what pride can lead to. He was consumed by jealousy and envy, which caused him to act irrationally. Pastor Elienai Cabral comments,

> Pride is an excessive sense of self-importance that prevents a person from engaging in self-criticism. It is a contagious disease that takes root in the heart, causing someone to lose the ability to recognize the existence and value of others. The lack of self-awareness leads them to act irrationally (Psalm 101:5; 2 Chronicles 26:16).[4]

At times, this kind of sin is not easily noticeable. It can disguise itself behind a humble and simple appearance. It can be hidden in people who seem "peaceful" and unwilling to stir up conflict. However, the heart is deceitful (Jer 17:9), and when we get to know such individuals, we may notice pride and arrogance deeply rooted in their hearts.

People like this are often highly critical of many things. They carry a sense of superiority, which leads them to avoid involvement because, according to them, "Everything is wrong anyway." We must constantly guard our hearts, making the same request as the psalmist: "Search me, God, and know my heart; test me and know my anxious thoughts. See if there is any offensive way in me, and lead me in the way everlasting" (Ps 139:23–24).

IF NOT ME

One of the dangers of a proud or arrogant heart is becoming entirely absorbed in what we do, which is not necessarily bad in itself), but becomes dangerous with an inner attitude that says "If not me, things won't happen." Sometimes, we may even endure

---

4. A soberba é o orgulho excessivo que uma pessoa demonstra e não tem nenhum senso de autocrítica. A soberba é uma doença contagiosa que se aloja no coração do homem e ele perde a capacidade de admitir que para viver no mundo dos homens ele precisa lembrar que o outro existe. A falta do senso de autocrítica o faz agir irracionalmente (Sl 101:5; 2 Cr 26:16). Cabral, *Integridade moral e espiritual*, 74.

suffering—or cause our family to suffer—just to be recognized and praised by others.

There are men and women of God who need to be mindful of the "if not me" attitude within the church. In every area of life, there are capable people who can contribute alongside us. This is not to say that you shouldn't strive for excellence in what you do—your dedication will highlight your strengths and bring good results. However, we must guard our hearts against the temptation of superiority and the need for recognition, even if it is disguised as humility. Let's not fall into temptations, in all its different forms.

FOR REFLECTION

1. What temptations have you been facing because of your own desires?
2. Do you recognize any sinful attitudes or behaviors in yourself that you need to abandon? What has this chapter taught you?

A PRAYER

Lord, forgive my sins. I don't want to make excuses—I simply acknowledge that I have failed. I need to take action so that sin will not have control over me. I ask for the power of the Holy Spirit to help me. I trust in you and in your forgiveness. In Jesus' name, amen!

6

What Is My Calling?

When I was a young Christian, I thought God kept His gifts on shelves, and the best gifts were on the highest shelves, so I had to reach up. Later, I discovered that the best gifts are on the lowest shelf, and I had to stoop down.

—D. L. Moody

Knowing that God has a calling for every Christian is a wonderful thing. The Lord distributes gifts according to his will through his "grace in its various forms." (1 Pet 4:10). However, discovering what my calling is can be a source of great anxiety. It becomes even more confusing when we use words like ministry, vocation, and God's will.

Calling, in Greek *klesis*, is a personal and individual invitation from God for you to carry out a specific task. It sounds simple, but do you know when and for what God is calling you? And if you are doing the right thing? Do you know if you are putting your gifts and talents into practice for the kingdom of God?

First of all, it is essential to clarify that it is completely normal to have these doubts when we want to serve the Lord with all our hearts. Some people quickly discover their gifts and develop them in God's house. That is wonderful! We see musicians who have been playing their instruments since childhood or adolescence, knowing that this is the ministry God has given them. Likewise, others sing in groups, choirs, or as soloists. And what a wonderful ministry that is! Everyone involved in music, from the sound technician to the lead singer, plays a significant role in the church. Others know their calling is in the word of God. Whether preaching or teaching, they do so with dedication, being used by God. However, some people do not discover their calling as easily. As mentioned earlier, God's manifold grace enables many other callings beyond singing or preaching in the church—callings that are just as essential as these.

A VARIETY OF CALLINGS

You may be called to serve, to pray, to evangelize, to support, to lead, or to organize. In practical terms, your calling might be visiting others, welcoming people in the reception, being part of a theater group, giving lectures, teaching Bible studies, writing, engaging in various art forms, organizing retreats and camps, planning leisure activities, visiting those in need, maintaining the church building, being part of chaplaincy, being a missionary in your own country or abroad, interceding for others, and more. The list could go on, and all of these callings have the same value in God's eyes.

We have unfortunately inherited the mistaken tradition that a calling is only for those who take the microphone. That is not true! In fact, as an anonymous pastor put it, "The pulpit is far too small for everyone to do God's work." Millions of Christians fulfill their callings without ever holding a microphone. Some callings are more visible simply due to their nature, but that does not mean they are more valuable than the work of a believer faithfully using the gift God has given them—even in complete anonymity.

What Is My Calling?

Let's highlight four fundamental aspects of discovering your calling in God's Kingdom.

1. Personal Calling

When we consider God's calling, I want to reference what he did in Moses' life. The book of Exodus shows us the Lord calling him: "When the Lord saw that he had gone over to look, God called to him from within the bush, 'Moses! Moses!' And Moses said, 'Here I am.'" (Exod 3:4). By looking at this beautiful story, we seek to understand the wonderful calling that God has for each of us.

First, we see that this was a *personal* calling. God called him by name. Have you ever stopped to think that God knows your name? You may be just one in eight billion people in this world, yet God knows you personally, and his calling is specific to your life.

The same thing happened with Jeremiah. God already had a specific plan for him even before he was born (Jer 1:5). While he was still in his mother's womb, the Lord had already set him apart for his work. In the New Testament, we see the example of Saul. On the road to Damascus, Jesus appeared to him, calling him by name as well. These are just a few examples in the Bible of God's personal calling in people's lives. Isn't it amazing to consider that God calls us personally?

2. Private Calling

I remember that as a teenager, and later as a young adult, I went to several retreats at the Word of Life camp, first as a camper, then as a staff member, and later as a leader. Many times, I would spend time alone with God. There were also moments outside of camp when I sought the Lord's presence in private. Those moments of fellowship with the Lord increasingly strengthened my conviction of his calling in my life.

Regarding biblical characters, Joe Jordan comments,

The privacy of the desert and Mount Horeb became God's megaphone for Moses. Was Moses the only one to have such an experience? No, Paul spent time alone with God in the Arabian desert. It was there that the apostle was instructed by the Lord regarding the specifics of his mission, message, and God's calling in his life.[1]

The same happened with Samuel and Mary. They were called by name for a specific purpose. God has a plan for each of us.

3. Purifying Calling

In addition to being personal and private, God's calling is *purifying*. God said to Moses, "Take off your sandals, for the place where you are standing is holy ground" (Exod 3:5).

God also set Jeremiah apart from his mother's womb. Paul used the same words regarding his calling: "But God . . . set me apart from my mother's womb" (Gal 1:15). The prophet Isaiah experienced purification in his calling when the angel touched his lips (Isa 6:7). This purified his lips and soul, propelling him to do the Lord's work.

I believe that knowing God has set you for a specific work contributes to purifying your life. Every aspect—your thoughts, words, and actions—will be refined, bringing a great transformation to your calling.[2]

4. Specific Calling

God has something *specific* for each of us. While he may use us in different areas, the way and purpose in which he calls us is unique—a designated task.

God's calling for Moses was tailor-made. He was chosen to lead the nation of Israel. The apostle Paul was called to preach to the gentiles. Esther was called to be the queen who would intercede

---

1. Jordan, *God*, 12.
2. Jordan, *God*, 13.

to prevent the extermination of the Jews in the Persian Empire. And the list goes on.

I know Pastor Jose Satirio dos Santos, whose calling was very specific—to start a missionary work in Colombia. You may be wondering, "But I've never had such a specific calling!" Perhaps your calling won't be exactly like these examples, and you may be used in different ministries. However, I believe that when you are available and walking at the center of God's will, he will guide you into his specific purpose for your life.

ANALYZE YOUR GIFTS, TALENTS, AND RESOURCES

It is important to distinguish between *gifts, talents, and resources.*

Gifts

These are the spiritual areas of life that God has given you. In Rom 12:6–8, Paul says,

> We have different gifts, according to the grace given to each of us. If your gift is prophesying, then prophesy in accordance with your faith; if it is serving, then serve; if it is teaching, then teach; if it is to encourage, then give encouragement; if it is giving, then give generously; if it is to lead, do it diligently; if it is to show mercy, do it cheerfully.

So, you may have received a gift from God to teach, preach, prophesy, lead, or contribute. Naturally, these gifts also need to be developed to be used more effectively.

Talents

These are physical and mental abilities that God has enabled you with. Some examples include working with children, mathematics, accounting, cooking, drawing, or sports. We all have some type of talent. It is amazing to see how many talents believers have that could be used in God's kingdom.

I remember a young woman who participated in a drama play with minimal rehearsals. It was clear to everyone that she had a talent for acting, which she later pursued in church performances after realizing it was part of her calling. I also recall youth bands that emerged, young leaders, and others who discovered their ability to communicate well. There is so much to be uncovered, especially among young people!

Resources

These are the physical and material things that God has given you to bless his work. This includes possessions, money, vehicles, homes, family, information, knowledge, and relationships. Your resources might be used beyond the church walls—there are countless possibilities out there. John Wesley, the English preacher responsible for one of the greatest revivals in England, once said, "I look upon all the world as my parish."[3]

So, use the resources God has given you to do something for his kingdom. The Salvation Army became one of the world's largest Christian charity organizations precisely because people decided that their resources could be channels of blessing to those in need.

IT'S NOT ALWAYS QUICK—DO WHAT COMES TO HAND

We don't always discover our calling quickly. Abraham only fully understood his calling when he had his promised son in his old age—at one hundred years old! Of course, it won't take you that long to find yours! But the truth is that many things may happen in your life before you become fully aware of what God specifically wants for you. Ecclesiastes 9:10 says, "Whatever your hand finds to do, do it with your might."

This means that you should do whatever comes your way, with your strength, even if it is not your ultimate calling. In fact,

---

3. Wesley, "Letters of John Wesley," Mar. 20.

these activities will serve as preparation for something greater. Many people want to be leaders or hold high positions but forget that everything starts small, often in obscurity. David faithfully tended his father's sheep with a heart of worship when no one was watching—but God saw him. That young shepherd became Israel's greatest king, and from his lineage came Jesus, whose throne will never end (2 Sam 7:12).

Samuel, who became the last judge and the first prophet of Israel, served in the temple as a teenager. The Bible tells us that he opened the doors, likely took care of the temple utensils, and helped in various tasks related to the ministry of the tabernacle. What an incredible example! A young man who started by simply opening the temple doors eventually received divine revelations and became God's representative to anoint Israel's kings. We could also mention Joshua, who served under Moses' leadership until he became his successor, leading Israel into the promised land.

Sadly, some believers refuse to do anything in the church, thinking certain tasks have "nothing to do" with them. They miss out on a great opportunity to discover their talents and serve in God's kingdom.

SERVE WITH JOY

One very important thing must not be forgotten, and Ps 100 reminds us of it: We must serve the Lord with joy. We cannot have the attitude of "I'm only doing this because my pastor keeps insisting"—absolutely not! Whatever we do in the church, even when it comes with responsibilities and difficulties, must be done with joy because we are serving God, not just people.

I have done many things in the church. I played the recorder, then the saxophone in the church band—those old-school marching bands! Later, I played bass guitar. Over time, I became more interested in God's word and started working with Bible studies for young people. Even though I didn't know exactly what my calling was, I helped my leaders with whatever they needed—organizing events, leading services. Later, I became a youth leader, Sunday school teacher, and began editing and translating Christian materials and writing, which also aligned with my professional background. Only after all this, God began speaking to me more clearly about giving me greater responsibilities. Throughout this entire process, God was shaping and equipping me to discover my calling and fully commit as an assistant pastor and teacher of the word.

BE READY WHEN HE CALLS

One thing is certain: God always takes the initiative when it comes to calling you. In John 15:16, Jesus said, "You did not choose me, but I chose you." The Lord calls each person as he wills. Remember Elisha, who was plowing the field when Elijah threw his cloak over him. We mentioned David, who was shepherding sheep when he was called to be anointed as Israel's king. Amos was a fig farmer and livestock caretaker when he was called to be a prophet. Although each had a specific calling, all of them came from God.

What truly matters is staying in fellowship with the Lord so that when he calls you, you are ready. When I say ready, I don't mean that you will feel capable—our ability comes from God. But you will know that he can use your life however he desires.

Think about Mary. Before becoming the mother of Jesus, she was just a simple, God-fearing young woman, living a devout and distinguished life. God saw something different in Mary—something he didn't see in other young women. Among all the women in the world, Mary was chosen to be the vessel through whom the Savior would come! As the writer Daniel Darling said,

> Mary was different from the others, not because of her outward appearance, but because of her inner spirit. The task of raising the Son of God could not be entrusted to someone irresponsible or careless. Mary was responsible, spiritual, and willing. She had all the qualities that made her the perfect candidate for this special mission.[4]

---

4. Darling, *Teen People*, 210.

Ultimately, it doesn't matter your background, skin color, gender, last name, social status, or connections to important people. What truly matters is whether your heart is turned toward God, if you have a willing spirit, and if you are committed to his word. If you have these qualities, you are a serious candidate for God to call you into a work that will bless lives, glorify his name, and give you the deep fulfillment of living out your purpose.

A CALLING FOR EVERYONE

There is a ministry that applies to all Christians. It does not depend on gifts or talents. This is the ministry of reconciliation. Paul speaks about this ministry:

> Therefore, if anyone is in Christ, the new creation has come: The old has gone, the new is here! All this is from God, who reconciled us to himself through Christ and gave us the ministry of reconciliation: that God was reconciling the world to himself in Christ, not counting people's sins against them. And he has committed to us the message of reconciliation. We are therefore Christ's ambassadors, as though God were making his appeal through us. We implore you on Christ's behalf: Be reconciled to God. God made him who had no sin to be sin for us, so that in him we might become the righteousness of God. (2 Cor 5:17–21)

We are all called to bring people back to God. Even though we may have specific callings, the Lord has given this ministry to everyone who is part of the church of Jesus Christ.

FOR REFLECTION

1. Are you making yourself available to the Lord to do whatever comes to your hands?
2. How could you further develop the ministry you are currently involved in?

A PRAYER

Lord, I want to live out your calling. Help me to understand and do whatever comes to my hands in your kingdom. Use me as an instrument in your hands to bring people to you. May I serve with joy, always glorifying your name! Amen.

7

Controlling Social Media

But the fruit of the Spirit is love, joy, peace, patience, kindness, goodness, faithfulness, gentleness and self-control. Against such things there is no law

—Gal 5:22–23

I'm trying to write this chapter about social media when suddenly I receive a text message. I could easily ignore it and check later, but that little notification sound triggers a mixed feeling of concern and curiosity, making it almost impossible to resist the temptation to check immediately. On top of that, as I attempt to write about technology, I feel even more drawn to glance at the seven unread emails I've received since yesterday. Actually, it's only three because four of them are just advertisements for something. And no matter how many times you unsubscribe from these unwanted email lists, they always find a way to reach you with something new—whether it's travel deals, services, products, spam, etc. Not to mention the constant temptation to take a quick peek at social media, in addition to the endless stream of information available online at any moment.

The reality is that we are being overwhelmed by virtual information! We often feel as if this force, greater than ourselves, is taking control of our behavior and thoughts. As anthropologist Juliano Spyer recently said in a podcast, "Our feeling is that whatever we have in relation to these technologies and social networks is never enough."[1] There's always something new being created, pressuring us to use it.

DEPENDENT

Today, if we are without our phones, we feel as if we were without clothes, not just in appearance but as if we are missing something we cannot live without. Being disconnected from the Internet and the world is entirely unimaginable. Owning a few computers at home, at least two televisions, and each person having their own cell phone is considered completely normal—or even the bare minimum. In fact, a friend of mine told me that his house has five televisions—one in the kitchen and even one in the bathroom!

WHY SO MUCH INFORMATION?

We are living in the era of the cyber revolution, the information age, or the digital generation. This moment in history began in the 1960s but has accelerated at an astonishing rate in recent years—it's the acceleration of acceleration. I clearly remember when I had no contact with computers, email, or social media. That was during my teenage years. But when I entered college, I had to create an email, and it felt like going to the moon! It was spectacular! Now, there are so many different options and communication channels that we are truly overwhelmed by such rapid advancements.

---

1. *Nossa sensação é a de que tudo que temos em relação a essas tecnologias e redes sociais não é suficiente.* Provoca, "Juliano Spyer compartilha," 1:06–1:15.

Daniel 12:4 says, "But you, Daniel, roll up and seal the words of the scroll until the time of the end. Many will go here and there to increase knowledge." This acceleration of knowledge and science was already prophesied. We have made more progress in these areas in the last twenty years than in the previous two thousand. Especially in the field of information technology, we can say that this process is irreversible—we cannot escape it. God has given humankind the ability to invent, evolve, and progress. This optimism toward progress has been present since the Renaissance in the sixteenth century, continuing through the Enlightenment and into the postmodern era we live in today, even though optimism has somewhat diminished. The information age is here, and while we can enjoy all its benefits, we are inevitably influenced by its negative aspects.

BENEFITS

The numerous benefits of technology and social media cannot be denied. There is no doubt that social networks have positive attributes. We can connect with distant family and friends we haven't been in touch with for a long time. Parents of children with autism spectrum disorder and mothers of newborns can be part of communities where they exchange experiences and provide mutual support, such as recommendations for services, professionals, and the sale of products of common interest. Prayer requests can be shared, and while some may not be moved, many others might be, leading to a collective effort in prayer for a specific cause or emergency.

When we upload photos from missionary trips or testify about God's blessings and miracles in our lives, we not only glorify the name of Jesus but also encourage others to dedicate themselves more to the Lord's work, strengthening their faith and trust in him who can do all things. Even for promoting church activities, social media has been essential due to its rapid dissemination and the increasing number of people connected who can access this information. Social media sites have also become important sources for consumers to learn more about products and services.

Recognizing this, companies use these platforms as an effective and low-cost marketing tool.

NEUTRALITY

Social media carries an element of neutrality. Just like a knife can be used to prepare a meal or harm someone; it is merely a tool—it can be used for good or for evil. But to what extent is it beneficial for a Christian to keep "scrolling" and staying "constantly connected" on social media? A guiding principle is found in 1 Cor 6:12—"'I have the right to do anything,' you say—but not everything is beneficial. 'I have the right to do anything'—but I will not be mastered by anything." Therefore, use the benefits of social media without allowing yourself to be *dominated* by it. Reject everything that is unworthy, such as engaging in posts that defame people, institutions, or pointless controversies.

While staying connected with people online can be beneficial, forming real-life relationships is even more important. About prioritizing in-person interactions over distant communication, the apostle John wrote: "Though I have much to write to you, I would rather not use paper and ink. Instead, I hope to come to you and talk face to face, so that our joy may be complete." (2 John 1:12 ESV). In this instance, the apostle chose not to use the technology of his time—paper and ink—to communicate with his brothers but rather to meet with them face to face. What a lesson!

PUBLIC AND DANGEROUS

Even those who are shy can easily express themselves through social media. This willingness to open up can indeed generate interest and friendships. However, expressing oneself or sharing personal aspects of life is not always positive. We must be aware that once we post something about ourselves, it becomes permanent and will be seen by more people than we might expect. It is often much better to share certain personal matters with a close friend in private. Moreover, the comments that arise from such posts can also be harmful, potentially creating controversy around a situation or even about yourself.

Another significant danger of social media is the inappropriate connections that can form between users. With the constant exposure, the sensuality displayed by many, and a general lack of caution, individuals in committed relationships are increasingly being lured into harmful interactions, often with devastating consequences for themselves and those around them. This kind of "cyber involvement" can seriously affect a believer's pursuit of holiness, leading to improper relationships, betrayals, and even divorce. We must remain vigilant against the temptations that arise through social media, remembering the words of Jesus: "The eye is the lamp of the body. If your eyes are healthy, your whole body will be full of light. But if your eyes are unhealthy, your whole body will be full of darkness." (Matt 6:22–23).

AN ANXIOUS GENERATION

One of the defining characteristics of this generation is anxiety. According to Gallup, the number of people with depression has reached the highest level in history.[2] Obviously, many factors contribute to this, but social media has played a significant role, especially among young people.

Social media has a reinforcing nature. Its use activates the brain's reward center, releasing dopamine, the "feel-good chemical" associated with pleasurable activities such as sex, food, and social interaction. These platforms are designed to be addictive and are linked to anxiety, depression, and even physical illnesses.

According to the Pew Research Center, 70 percent of adults and 85 percent of teenagers in the United States use social media. This places a significant portion of the population at an increased

---

2. Witters, "U.S. Depression Rates."

risk of feeling anxious, depressed, or even physically unwell due to social media use.[3]

One of the effects of anxiety disorders is a lack of concentration. Social media directly influences this because it serves as pastime in an attempt to ease their apprehension. When individuals feel dissatisfied with their daily activities, social media becomes an escape from reality. However, studies show that excessive use of social media and information consumption often triggers what people least want—an increase in anxiety.

This rise in anxiety is largely due to something people naturally do while using social media—comparison. When scrolling through social networks and seeing others happy, enjoying life, always smiling, and accomplishing great things, the immediate reaction is to compare it to one's own situation. *Why can't I do the same?* Even if this comparison happens subconsciously, it still affects stress and anxiety levels.

In his book *Imperfeitos, livres, e felizes* (*Imperfect, Free, and Happy*) psychiatrist Christophe André states,

> The conscious and relentless desire to always showcase the best version of ourselves and to perfectly control how others perceive us—constantly monitoring for the slightest misunderstanding or flaw in our image—becomes a significant source of stress.[4]

STIMULUS-DRIVEN GENERATION

The expansion of knowledge and technology has turned us into stimulus-driven people. We have access to so many things at once. At home, simply watching TV is no longer enough—many now watch TV with their phone in hand, while others go even further,

---

3. McLean Hospital, "Scrolling and Stress."

4. *Seja como for, o desejo consciente e desenfreado de estar sempre mostrando o melhor de nós mesmos e de controlar perfeitamente a maneira como somos vistos (estar sempre espreitando o menor mal-entendido ou o menor defeito na imagem que os outros podem ter de nós) representa efetivamente uma considerável fonte de estresse.* André, *Imperfeitos, livres, e felizes*, 211.

using both a smartphone and an open laptop at the same time. So, while all this technology has brought countless benefits—connecting us with everything and everyone simultaneously—it has also made us dependent on it. We can no longer live without the constant stimulation of checking the news, messages, posts, likes, and more.

Parents around the world are concerned, and even comedy movies (*Grown Ups*, for example) depict how children no longer play outside. They don't know how to or simply don't want to do anything outdoors because they are so obsessed with video games, tablets, and other devices. The way children and teenagers have fun today is vastly different from a few years ago. There are fewer people outside, especially in big cities. Technology and social media are suffocating us. They steal precious time that we could be using for more meaningful and enjoyable activities.

GUARDIANS

In a sense, we are all guardians. Like watchmen, we monitor what we see, hear, and think. We are responsible for what enters our minds through our ears and eyes and settles into our hearts. Therefore, we must spend more time in the "Faith Book" (the holy Scriptures) and less on Facebook. Only when we read this word do we receive direction for our path (Isa 30:21); when we know this word, we do not go astray (Matt 22:29); when we meditate on this word day and night, we are blessed (Ps 1:2); and when we store it in our hearts, we do not sin against the Lord (Ps 119:11). Charles Swindoll expresses this well when he says, "The precepts and principles of the Bible reach fibers that no scalpel or surgeon can touch—the soul, the spirit, thoughts, attitudes, and the very essence of our being."[5]

---

5. Swindoll, *Strengthening Your Grip*, 77.

MAKING THE MOST OF TIME

Paul warns us in Eph 5:15–16: "See then that you walk circumspectly, not as fools but as wise, redeeming the time, because the days are evil." (NKJV). The word "redeeming" in the original Greek (*eksagoradzō*) means "to rescue from loss or harm." In other words, when we redeem our time, we are protecting it from being wasted or causing us harm. Let's be honest—our days go by quickly due to our many responsibilities. The time we have left should be wisely spent with our family, church, personal time with God, or in real-world relationships. Time flies when we are "hypnotized" in front of a computer, and what should be dedicated to truly important things is often pushed aside.

Nowadays, there are already studies and research on what is called "Social Media Addiction." Neuropsychologist Nivashinie Mohan from Gleneagles Hospital in Malaysia states, "This disorder often goes undetected because most addicts do not realize or do not want to admit they have a problem."[6] This is truly difficult—acknowledging that we have an addiction. However, it is possible to break free and live the life that God intends for us.

OVERINDULGING IN APPETIZERS

Pastor and author Stan Toler describes how we often fill up on appetizers at a restaurant, so by the time the main course arrives, we are too full to enjoy it. He says,

> I love Mexican restaurants. Most of them serve a basket of crispy tortilla chips with a variety of salsas to whet the appetite. But more than once, I have sat down, placed my order, and then, by the time my food arrived, I realized I had eaten so many chips that I was no longer hungry! Taking this restaurant analogy in a slightly different direction, most of us wouldn't sit at a restaurant table and refuse to order from the menu. When the waiter asks, "How may I serve you?" we don't just say, "Bring me any

---

6. Lim, "Making Connections That Matter."

> reheated leftovers. Surprise me." Not at all. We want to spend money on something we know we will enjoy. Unfortunately, most of us tend to be far less disciplined and selective when it comes to consuming media. We sit in front of the television, the computer, or open a magazine or book, and by our actions, we are essentially saying, "Surprise me." Instead of snacking lightly and moving on to a well-balanced social, intellectual, and spiritual meal, we overindulge in appetizers. Then, by the time we look away from the cellphone, computer or TV screen, we realize it's already past bedtime, and we haven't taken in the real nourishment we needed.[7]

How often do we do this? Instead of focusing on what is truly beneficial, we spend so much time on electronic distractions—many of which provide entertainment that corrodes our spiritual lives.

CONTROLLING YOUR MEDIA CONSUMPTION

There's no use in longing for the pre-internet days when people spent time chatting with their neighbors, children had no electronic entertainment, and life seemed simpler—and how happy we were. The Bible itself warns us against this mindset: "Do not say, 'Why were the old days better than these?' For it is not wise to ask such questions" (Eccl 7:10) There's no point in being nostalgic about these things, as there is no going back from the digital era we live in. We will have more and more access to technology and media. What we need is stronger control over our media consumption, with discipline and the guidance of the Holy Spirit.

Here are some tips on how to manage your media consumption effectively:

1. **Plan.** Evaluate your engagement with different types of media and identify what you would like to change. Ask yourself: What should I stop accessing?

---

7. Toler, *ReThink Your Life*, 78–79.

2. **Set time limits.** Define how much time you will spend on media. For example, decide to check social media only in the morning and late afternoon. This helps you stay focused on other important things.
3. **Take a media fast.** You don't need to start with a long period—begin with a single day and gradually increase it. Soon, you'll realize you can go longer without it, and it won't feel like a loss.
4. **Engage with people.** Many people are feeling lonely and are waiting for your presence and attention.

A PRAYER

Lord, help me to have control over my use of social media. May the precious time you have given me be used wisely. Help me focus on the responsibilities you have entrusted to me so that I am not distracted by so much information that does not add value to my life. May my greatest joy be in fellowship with you, in your word, and in doing your will. In Jesus' name, amen!

8

Taking Care of My Body

Take care of your body as if you were going to live forever; and take care of your soul as if you were going to die tomorrow.

—Saint Augustine

A quick Google search using the words "woman" and "beauty" returns nearly twenty-seven million results—proof of how much attention this topic receives! The pressure society places on women to meet certain beauty standards is intense. And let's not forget—men also face increasing pressure in this image-driven culture.

But is there really anything wrong with wanting to look good or stay in shape? For those of us who follow the Bible as our guide for faith and daily living, how should we approach this?

In this chapter, we'll explore some key perspectives on how we view our bodies and physical appearance through the lens of our faith.

BODY—TEMPLE OF THE HOLY SPIRIT? WHAT DOES THAT MEAN?

Yes, you have probably heard this many times before, as it is indeed in the Bible, specifically in 1 Cor 6:19. Paul says, "Do you not know that your bodies are temples of the Holy Spirit, who is in you, whom you have received from God? You are not your own."

We are the masterpiece of God's creation. He created everything through his word, but we, human beings, were made with his own hands, shaped in his image and likeness (Gen 1:26). For this reason alone, it would be enough motivation for us to take good care of the body that God created through the original couple.

However, Paul goes even further in the New Testament when he states that our body is the dwelling place of the Holy Spirit. This Holy Spirit residing in us is something unique to the new covenant in Christ—and this is only possible because we have a physical body for him to dwell in. That is, the Holy Spirit does not just roam around in the air; he lives inside every true Christian (John 14:27). That is why the same apostle Paul tells us to flee from impurity, for every sin we commit is outside the body, but when we practice immorality, we sin against our own body (1 Cor 6:18). And in another verse, he asks whether our body, which is a member of Christ, can be united with a prostitute (1 Cor 6:15). Of course not!

THIS BODY WILL BE TRANSFORMED

We need to let go of the idea that this body is worthless, that Jesus is coming just for our souls and that's it! In fact, once again, Paul teaches us that it is *this very body* that will be transformed at the rapture. Think about it—if our bodies weren't important, why would Jesus come to retrieve us in our *physical* bodies, and not just our souls, on that great day? Even those who have already died in the Lord—who are not yet in their final state in heaven—will return to their bodies, and then we will all be transformed into glorified bodies as we meet Jesus in the air (1 Cor 6:14; 1 Thess 3:16).

So we must take care of our bodies. Christian writer James Bryan Smith puts it this way:

> What does this have to do with Christian spiritual formation? Human beings are not just souls housed in bodies. Our body and soul are integrated. If our body suffers, our soul suffers too. We cannot neglect the body in our pursuit of spiritual growth. In fact, neglecting our body will inevitably hinder our spiritual growth. Everything we do in life—including spiritual formation practices—we do in and with our body. If our body is not well-rested, our energy will be low, and our ability to pray, read the Bible, spend time in solitude, or memorize Scripture will be diminished.[1]

I can speak from experience—when I'm not physically well, it directly affects my spiritual life.

SOME PEOPLE EAT A LOT!

Well, another word for eating too much is *gluttony*. It's easy for us to view drinking and smoking as sin, along with stealing, adultery, and so on. But rarely do we consider overeating a sin. Generally, we ignore or tolerate it—and even joke about it. Many Christians wouldn't even consider drinking a beer or smoking a cigarette, yet won't think twice about devouring everything in front of them.

Proverbs 23:20–21 says, "Do not join those who drink too much wine or gorge themselves on meat, for drunkards and gluttons become poor, and drowsiness clothes them in rags." Here we see the first danger—becoming such a glutton that you spend a good portion of your resources on it and end up in financial trouble; or becoming lazy and unmotivated due to the drowsiness and fatigue that overeating brings, which can prevent you from doing what's necessary.

Proverbs 23:2 also says, "Put a knife to your throat if you are given to gluttony." This is very similar to what Jesus said when he

---

1. Smith, *Good and Beautiful God*, 42.

spoke of cutting off your hand if it causes you to sin—better to enter heaven with one hand than be cast out with both.

There is no doubt that overeating harms the body. It's well established that gluttony is the primary cause of health issues for many who are obese. And obese individuals suffer in countless ways, being more prone to various diseases. So, if our body is the temple of the Holy Spirit, and overeating causes harm to it, then that is sin.

Lack of control over eating is a lack of self-control, which is one of the virtues of the fruit of the Spirit (Gal 5). If a Christian lacks self-control when it comes to eating, it's likely they struggle with it in other areas as well. And the fruit of the Spirit is something every believer is called to bear.

If you've been sinning in this area and harming your body, it's time to stop. Don't cast your anxiety onto food—cast your anxiety onto Jesus. Peter reminds us, "Cast all your anxiety on him because he cares for you" (1 Pet 5:7).

MOVE YOURSELF

I believe there isn't anyone who does not know the benefits of physical activity. It doesn't matter whether it's going to the gym, walking, playing soccer, running, weight training, cycling, swimming, or any other form of exercise. Physical activity not only burns fat but has also been proven to benefit the heart, circulation, and overall physical and emotional well-being. People with diabetes, for example, can greatly benefit from exercise.

The most common excuse for not engaging in any physical activity is that "I don't have time!" The problem is that many people, especially believers, see physical activity as just an extra activity, a leisure pursuit—not as fundamental as working, studying, or church. The mindset is, if I can do it, great; if I can't, it's not essential! However, physical activity should be viewed as just as fundamental as these other essential aspects of life. As I mentioned, I am taking care of the temple of the Holy Spirit, and I should glorify God through my body. If we only do this when we have time, we will never do it. But when we truly want to do something, we find the time for it. It's a matter of priorities.

We need to give proper value to taking care of our bodies. Once, I told a young church worker—who was exhausted, stressed, and dealing with health issues—that if he didn't take care of himself, his ministry might end sooner than God intended. Of course, even when we do everything we can, we are not exempt from illnesses, the natural consequences of aging, emotional pressures, or genetic predispositions to certain diseases. But what we *can* do is our responsibility, and doing so will certainly help us live a healthier life that pleases God. Much has been said about how God is looking for people who are willing to *die* for him. I would say that God is even more interested in people who are willing to *live* for him! And he wants that from you too.

BEAUTY

In this section, I will primarily address women. I want to share a bit of Regina Franklin's story. She says that as a child, she was always enchanted by beauty pageants and all their glamour. She imagined herself one day walking the runway like those women. It is true that most young girls see themselves as the stars of their own show, the princesses of their own kingdoms. These childhood dreams are part of life at that stage, but eventually, they begin to learn the difference between reality and illusion.

However, Regina says that the *myth of beauty* lingers long after childhood. This fascination with the princess myth is problematic because it shifts the focus from a mere description to the central theme—physical beauty becomes the defining message of one's life story rather than just a detail. The idea of a man willing to risk his life for his beloved is reduced to stories of maidens being rescued solely because of their exceptional beauty. This can lead to much frustration, especially for girls, because we live in a world where physical appearance is still heavily emphasized.

From movie stars who try to convince us that happiness and success are exclusive rewards for fitting into this stereotype, to social media and television, everything reinforces the pressure to be thinner, younger, and better. Regina describes this overwhelming pressure on women:

> We face a daily bombardment of images portraying perfection from a single point of view. Gradually, these images become our reality. We forget that these photos were created to sell products. Desiring acceptance from those around us, we go to great lengths to attain the appearance the world tells us we must have. From endless diets to drastic cosmetic surgeries, from creams to pills, from clothes to shoes, we keep trying to reshape ourselves according to the world's image of perfection.[2]

Regina also points out that what is culturally accepted as beautiful is often achieved only through a combination of photo editing, camera angles, lighting, and heavy use of Photoshop—creating illusions that seem almost miraculous. She recalls an actress from a TV series who, despite being portrayed as an ordinary housewife, looked far from average. In an interview, the actress openly admitted to undergoing plastic surgery, including a tummy tuck and a breast lift. Then, she pulled out a plastic bag labeled "snack" full of pills. "This one," she said, "helps metabolize fat, and this one suppresses appetite." Although this isn't the norm for everyone, she continued to perpetuate the ideal of beauty.[3]

The truth is, many women work tirelessly to conform to a beauty standard dictated by popular culture. Christian girls and women are no exception. Unfortunately, when the desire to fit the world's standards becomes more important than aligning with God's standards, this battle will never be won. We cannot disregard beauty or the pursuit of it—denying that would be hypocritical. The Bible itself shows us that Esther's beauty caught the eye of King Ahasuerus, and she won his favor, leading her to be chosen as queen. Many Christian women overlook this, believing that only spiritual matters are important. However, beyond Esther's physical beauty, what truly set her apart was that she was not seduced by vanity or

---

2. Franklin, *Who Calls Me Beautiful?*, 11.
3. Franklin, *Who Calls Me Beautiful?*, 52.

superficiality. Sadly, many women, including Christian women, are engaged in an eager pursuit of beauty without demonstrating the same dedication to cultivating more significant virtues.

WHO IS THIS WOMAN?

I once heard a sister say that just reading about the virtuous woman of Prov 31 made her feel exhausted! The qualities of that woman seem almost unreal. She is a devoted mother who "rises while it is yet night and provides food for her household" (Prov 31:15a ESV). She manages multiple household tasks (Prov 31:15b), provides clothing for her children, and "is not afraid of snow for her household, for all her household are clothed in scarlet" (Prov 31:21 ESV). This woman educates her children with wisdom and kindness (Prov 31:26), anticipates domestic challenges, and "does not eat the bread of idleness" (Prov 31:27). As an entrepreneur, she buys fabric and makes garments, bedspreads, and linens (Prov 31:13, 22). She engages in trade and manages profitable businesses (Prov 31:14, 16). She is generous, extending her hands to the poor and needy (Prov 31:20). Douglas Baptista comments,

> Indeed, biblically, this woman is strong and prosperous, but she is also generous and compassionate toward the poor and needy (Prov. 31:20). She is full of energy, has good character, and is confident about the future (Prov. 31:25). This woman—wife, mother, and entrepreneur— is praised by her family (Prov. 31:28-29). Her immeasurable worth does not reside in her physical appearance but in a heart that fears the Lord (Prov. 31:30). The example and virtues of this woman will be publicly recognized (Prov. 31:31).[4]

---

4. *De fato, biblicamente, essa mulher é aguerrida e próspera, mas também é generosa e sensível na ajuda aos pobres e necessitados (Pv 31:20). Ele é cheia de energia e de bom caráter e é autoconfiante em relação ao futuro (Pv 31:25). Essa mulher, esposa, mãe e empreendedora é louvada pela sua família (Pv 31:28, 29). O seu valor imensurável não reside na aparência física, mas num coração temente a Deus, o Senhor (Pv 31:30). O exemplo e as virtudes dessa mulher serão publicamente reconhecidos (Pv 31:31).* Baptista, *Igreja de Cristo*, 86.

THE LUST OF THE EYES

Eve saw that the fruit was good to eat. The word of God says it was "pleasing to the eye" (Gen 3:6). Similarly, Jesus was tempted in this sense when Satan tried to convince him to throw himself down from the pinnacle of the temple (Matt 4:6). Satan told Jesus that it was written that his angels would catch him so that no harm would come to him.

Notice how Satan has always distorted the truth. In this passage, he twists Ps 91—a promise of lasting provision and protection—into something for Jesus to claim for himself, bringing glory to himself and fulfilling Satan's deceptive purposes.

Likewise, Satan wants to use our bodies, especially women's bodies, for his purposes rather than God's. We live in a visually driven culture where images provoke reactions. When a woman strives to attain worldly beauty, she takes what God intended to be a vessel of honor and instead uses it to glorify herself—to be admired and desired—thus leading to the lust of the eyes. *The New Biblical Commentary* defines the lust of the eyes as "a strong desire for what is seen, for the outward appearance of things. It is the craving for the superficial."[5]

The pursuit of worldly beauty is rarely motivated by a desire to glorify God. More often, it stems from the longing to be "pleasing to the eye" (Gen 3:6). A pastor once addressed the women serving on his church's worship team about their attire for church services. He said he wouldn't lay out a list of rules but instead asked them to consider one simple question: "When you dress to come and minister in church, are you dressing to be admired, or are you dressing to glorify God?" With that, he concluded the conversation.

It is simply not acceptable for Christian women to wear indecent clothing or post sensual photos on social media that stir up lustful desires in men. God has not called women to this; he has called them to be vessels of honor, bringing glory to him through their bodies. Men, too, must be cautious not to expose themselves by wearing tight or revealing clothing just to keep

---

5. Guthrie et al., *New Bible Commentary*, 821.

up with fashion trends. Paul's words should serve as a principle for all of us in how we present and care for our bodies: "For God gave us a spirit not of fear but of power and love and self-control" (2 Tim 1:7 ESV). Self-control brings balance—it is the mastery of one's desires and the rejection of excess. When it comes to our bodies, the goal is not to idolize them but to care for them as instruments for the glory of God.

FOR REFLECTION

1. Excesses regarding our bodies can be harmful to our lives. What excesses have you struggled with in taking care of your body?
2. How could you improve in this area?

A PRAYER

Lord, you have wonderfully created me. My body belongs to you. I do not want to be influenced by the culture of body worship, but I also do not want to neglect proper care of my body. I want to strive to live a healthy life as much as it depends on me until you call me home. May my body be an instrument in your hands for your glory!

9

My Children, My Inheritance

Each day of our lives we make deposits into the memory banks of our children.

—Charles Swindoll

A WELL-KNOWN PASSAGE IN the Bible states that children are an inheritance from the Lord. This is recorded in Ps 127:3. The word "inheritance" refers to something that will be given to you in the future. Unfortunately, we also see how inheritance has caused disputes, conflicts, and divisions within families. Normally, an inheritance is claimed after the death of the parents. In the case of the Parable of the Prodigal Son, we read the sad account of the son asking for his inheritance while his father was still alive (Luke 15:11–32).

However, God's word says that children will not become an inheritance, but they already are the inheritance of the Lord for their parents. They are a gift, a present—not from human beings, but from the Lord himself. The inheritance that our earthly parents can leave us may be a blessing in our lives, but I believe that God's inheritance that is our children is much greater.

INHERITANCE—A BLESSING OR A PROBLEM?

It is important to explore the concept of inheritance in more depth. If we study the Old Testament, we see that having a large family was considered a blessing. On the other hand, not having children was viewed as a curse. The story of Hannah, as told in 1 Sam 1, shows the distress she experienced because she was unable to bear children.

In the New Testament or new covenant, having many children is not necessarily evidence of divine favor, and not being able to have children does not mean divine punishment. When it comes to having children, the key issue is how we handle the inheritance we receive. An inheritance left by parents can be a source of conflict if it is not managed correctly among those who are entitled to it—typically, the siblings. Similarly, there will be discord and strain in handling the inheritance from the Lord if there is no harmony between the parents.

In this regard, we can say that the way we treat this inheritance—how we raise our children—will be a decisive factor in whether it becomes a blessing or not. This leads us to reflect on the next topic.

HARMONY AMONG HEIRS

Sadly, inheritance often becomes a source of family conflict and division. Yet the true issue is not the inheritance itself, but the lack of harmony among the heirs. When love and respect are missing, and materialism and greed take root, relationships suffer deep wounds. The Bible illustrates this through the story of Jacob deceiving his brother Esau over their inheritance (Gen 27).

If parents are not united—spiritually, emotionally, and physically—their children will inevitably feel the consequences. The prophet Amos asks, "Do two walk together unless they have agreed to do so?" (Amos 3:3). A lack of intimacy is one of the greatest threats to any marriage. Christian writer and psychologist Neil Warren notes, "If two people do not know each other deeply, they may never become what the Bible calls 'one flesh.' They will never be truly 'joined,' 'united,' 'fused,' or 'welded together.'"[1]

This absence of intimacy often leads to disunity in parenting, with each parent thinking and acting independently. As a result, children are left confused, lacking clear and consistent guidance from both parents.

For this reason, it is crucial that Christian parents deepen their relationship with the Lord. As they grow spiritually, their unity in marriage will be strengthened, and this will profoundly impact how they raise and lead their children.

THE PRIMARY MISSION

Every baby that comes into the world, with an immortal soul, holds immense value in the eyes of God. However, all children are descendants of Adam. As precious and beautiful as they are, they are born in sin and possess a sinful nature. David acknowledged this: "Surely I was sinful at birth, sinful from the time my mother conceived me" (Ps 51:5). Paul also addresses this in his Letter to the Romans: "Therefore, just as sin entered the world through one man, and death through sin, and in this way death came to all people, because all sinned" (Rom 5:12).

Given this reality, the primary mission of parents is to lead their children to Jesus Christ. The role of parents is to raise their children to become part of God's people, with heaven as their ultimate goal. This task requires effort, sacrifice of time and energy, and a deep commitment. Parents must see this as their foremost mission on earth, alongside maintaining their fellowship with the Lord and strengthening one another. It is incredibly worthwhile to set the goal of raising children to become men and women of God, filled with the Holy Spirit. It is tragic when parents provide

---

1. Warren, *Love of Your Life*, 117.

their children with so many material things but fail in their most important responsibility—guiding them in faith. The apostle John expressed that nothing brought him greater joy than knowing his spiritual children were walking in the truth: "I have no greater joy than to hear that my children are walking in the truth" (3 John 4).

BEING AN EXAMPLE FOR YOUR CHILDREN

From a very young age, children observe everything their parents do. I remember a time when I ran a red light, and my son Daniel, who was little at the time, said, "Dad, you went through a red light." I had to admit my mistake because I had enough time to stop. It is natural for children to imitate their parents, both in good and bad actions. The Gospel of Matthew recounts that when Jesus entered Jerusalem, the crowds shouted, "Hosanna to the Son of David!" A little later, in the temple, the children echoed the same words—"Hosanna to the Son of David!"—even though they did not fully understand their meaning (Matt 21:9, 15–16).

Paul instructed Titus to teach young men to be self-controlled and to be an example for them himself (Titus 2:6–7). Parents are the greatest influence in a child's life. Their impact is far greater than that of teachers, pastors, or other authority figures. While these individuals can certainly shape a child's life, the example set by parents is the most powerful.

That is why parents must be the first to demonstrate prayer, Bible reading, and genuine spirituality at home. Every household, even those of faithful believers, faces struggles and challenges. There is no perfect home, but what children need to see in their parents is consistency in their spiritual lives—where principles are not compromised, forgiveness is practiced, and God is glorified. The parents of Moses were such a strong example for him in the short time they raised him that even after years of living in the pharaoh's palace, he chose to suffer and follow the God of his parents rather than enjoy the pleasures of Egypt (Heb 11:24–26).

TEACHING ALONG THE WAY

Regarding the upbringing of children, Prov 22:6 gives an important exhortation to parents: "Start children off on the way they should go, and even when they are old they will not turn from it." Today, we see many parents wanting to *point* their children to the right path while they themselves are not walking in it. Some parents think it is good for their child to go to church, yet they do not attend themselves. I have seen parents drop off their children—whether kids or teenagers—at church, Sunday school, or other services, only to pick them up at the end. One might argue that at least they are bringing their children to church, which is good, but the verse says parents should train their children *in* the way—not just show them *the* way. The impact is entirely different when parents lead by example. As writer Daniel Darling puts it, "Because of Saul's sin, Jonathan lost the opportunity to be the next king of Israel."[2]

PURPOSE IN EDUCATION

Parents must examine, with reverence before the Lord, their goals in educating their children. They need to reflect on whether their aspirations for their children align with God's will or if they are merely fulfilling their own ambitions. Some parents project onto their children what they are or what they wished to have been. For example, just because a father is a lawyer, he should not pressure his child to follow the same career path solely to satisfy his personal desires. Children often choose professions different from those their parents envisioned, and this must be respected, considering their aptitudes, talents, and aspirations.

Lamech's children, descendants of Cain, are examples of "successful" individuals who excelled in various fields. Jabal was the father of those who dwelled in tents and raised livestock. Jubal pioneered music and the arts. Tubal-Cain became a skilled craftsman of metal tools, laying the foundation for industry. They were

---

2. Darling, *Teen People*, 142.

instrumental in shaping civilization, yet their lineage was completely estranged from God (Gen 4). Jacob Graf comments, "The world without God offers everything that can satisfy the natural heart, including success, but it is a system that ultimately leads to judgment."[3] Unfortunately, this pursuit of success has significantly influenced Christians, often harming their spiritual journey. In contrast, in Gen 4, Adam and Eve had another son, Seth, whose son Enosh was born during a time when people began to call on the name of the Lord (Gen 4:17–26).

There is nothing wrong with striving to provide a good education, career opportunities, and a stable future for children. Parents should encourage their growth and development. However, this should never come at the cost of weakening their children's spiritual lives. Rather than nurturing hearts softened by God's presence, some parents unknowingly foster materialistic mindsets focused only on achievements and success. They prioritize secular ambitions over a committed relationship with a local church. Sadly, in the name of "chasing dreams" and "stability," many fall into this pattern. May God protect us, granting wisdom and grace to guide our children ever closer to him.

WHAT RITE IS THIS?

Exodus 12:26–27 records that Israelite children would one day ask about the ritual of placing lamb's blood on the doorposts and lintels of their houses. The parents were to respond, "It is the Passover sacrifice to the Lord, who passed over the houses of the Israelites in Egypt and spared our homes when he struck down the Egyptians" (Exod 12:27). This was a significant opportunity for parents to teach their children about God's deliverance and his judgment upon those who sought their destruction.

Likewise, as parents today, we have many opportunities to teach our children about the meaning of the Lord's Supper, the

---

3. *O mundo sem Deus oferece tudo o que pode satisfazer o coração natural, oferece também o sucesso, mas é um sistema cujo fim desemboca no juízo.* Graf, *Falando francamente*, 75.

elements of our worship services, and the significance of water baptism. As commentator Russell Shedd notes, "Every worship service, every rite, every sacrament is intended to teach God's Word, to instruct participants about what God has done, commanded, and promised."[4]

Different moments in daily life can serve as opportunities to share God's word. As instructed in Deut 11:19, parents should teach their children about God *at home, on the road, in the morning, and at night*. I realized that the simple act of driving my children to school could be a meaningful time to listen to God's word. And so it has been.

PERSONAL CHOICES

It is important to remember that, ultimately, we are all responsible for our own choices. While parents bear a great responsibility in raising their children, each child must eventually choose their own path. Some parents blame themselves and wonder where they went wrong when they see their children drifting away from the Lord. In some cases, parents may indeed have influenced this outcome—whether through hypocritical legalism at home, a lack of discipline, or the absence of clear boundaries. However, this is not always the case. The story of Samson, as told in Judg 13–16, illustrates this reality. Samson's parents were a God-fearing couple who were blessed with a miraculous child destined to be a leader in Israel. They faithfully followed the angel's instructions, raising him according to God's law. As he grew, Samson was blessed by the Lord (Judg 13:24). However, despite his upbringing, Samson made his own disastrous choices, disregarding his parents' wisdom.

---

4. *Cada culto, cada rito, cada sacramento tem a finalidade de ensinar a palavra de Deus, instruir os participantes nas coisas que Deus tem feito, ordenado e prometido.* Shedd, *Bíblia Shedd*, 90.

THE PRODIGAL SON

Like Samson's story, the Parable of the Prodigal Son (Luke 15) also highlights the truth that, as children grow, their decisions ultimately become their own responsibility. From the text, we understand that the prodigal son had a loving father, yet he chose to squander his life and resources. In fact, the term *prodigal* means someone who recklessly wastes their possessions—one who is extravagant and wasteful.

When children are young, parents have more control over their lives. However, as they reach adolescence and young adulthood, new challenges arise. Independence of thought, relationships, external influences, and other factors begin to shape their choices, sometimes leading to both missteps and growth. I, too, experienced a period in my youth when I strayed from the Lord. Yet, through God's grace and the intercession of my parents and many others, I had a life-changing encounter with Christ. The example of the prodigal son's father is one that parents should follow—he never stopped loving, never lost hope, and rejoiced upon his son's return. This father is, in fact, a reflection of our heavenly Father, who loves us unconditionally and longs for an intimate relationship with us.

PRAYING FOR OUR CHILDREN

I always tell parents that if there is one prayer God hears, it is the prayer of parents. Of course, this is a figure of speech, as God hears all prayers made with a sincere heart. But what I want to emphasize is that, generally, a parent's heart is solely focused on ardently desiring the well-being of their children. And God knows this. It is a privilege to entrust our children and their challenges at each stage of life to the Lord. In the New Testament, we have four accounts of how the prayers of suffering parents for their children were answered.

1. **Jairus' daughter.** Jairus, a leader in the synagogue, had a daughter who was dying. He came to Jesus, fell at his feet, and pleaded for his daughter. On the way to the girl, Jesus was delayed by another situation, and the child died. The father was encouraged by Jesus, who went to the house and resurrected the girl (Mark 5:21–43).

2. **The Canaanite woman.** A Canaanite woman had to persist in prayer because she was outside the limits of Israel and the "blessings" of the Lord. But her persistence was remarkable, even when Jesus tested her faith. She made brief yet powerful supplications: "Lord, Son of David, have mercy on me!" and "Lord, help me!" Amazed by the mother's faith, Jesus healed her daughter (Matt 15:21–28).

3. **The royal official's son.** The son of a royal official was sick in Capernaum. The father heard that Jesus was in the region and begged him to heal his son: "Sir, come down before my child dies." Jesus responded, "Go . . . your son will live." The man believed Jesus' word. His son was healed (John 4:46–54).

4. **The demon-possessed boy.** A desperate father brought his son, who was suffering from seizures, to Jesus' disciples, but they were unable to cast out the demon. The father then went to Jesus, knelt before him, and pleaded, "Lord, have mercy on my son . . . he . . . is suffering greatly" (Matt 17:15). Jesus had compassion and cast out the demon from the child.

These four stories show us how Jesus responded to the cries of parents for their children. The author of Hebrews reminds us that we do not have a high priest who is unable to empathize with us (Heb 4:15). Human help may fail, but the Lord's help never does. Many times, he does not respond in the way we desire, for he acts with wisdom, aiming to glorify his name. However, I have heard many testimonies of parents who prayed for their children, and even though time passed, God acted. Parents with children who are not believers or who have drifted away should always pray for their spiritual restoration, as this is God's will.

My Children, My Inheritance

Our children are a precious inheritance. May God grant us grace, wisdom, authority, and great love to care for them and bring them ever closer to an intimate relationship with the Lord.

FOR REFLECTION

1. How has your spiritual influence impacted your children?
2. What practical steps can you take to bring your children closer to the Lord?

A PRAYER

Lord, I thank you and praise you for the children you have given me. They are a blessing in my life. I ask for your presence in their lives. May they have real experiences with you. Increase their faith and hunger for your word. Help me to be the father or mother that you want me to be for them. My desire is to be a channel of your grace and love in their lives. Amen.

10

Finding Satisfaction in My Work

No good work is done anywhere without the help of the Father of Lights.
—C. S. Lewis

WHY WORK?

ONE OF THE THINGS God gave man to do on this earth is work. Even before the fall, God had already commanded Adam to cultivate and care for the garden of Eden. However, to take care of a garden of that size, man possessed immense strength. After the fall, work changed its focus—now it would be through sweat and toil that we would obtain our sustenance (Gen 3:17–19). However, since man became inherently sinful due to disobedience, work is a great activity that God left us so that we would not occupy our time with wicked things.

The apostle Paul also gives another reason for working: "If anyone is not willing to work, let him not eat" (2 Thess 3:10 ESV).

Well, that is a good reason to work—I need to eat. The Bible also contains other passages that value work and rebuke the lazy person who refuses to work (Prov 6:6–8; 10:4–5; 20:13; Eccl 10:18).

I tell young people that if they can balance work and education, they should do so. Whether it's an internship or a part-time job, especially if it is in their field of interest, it can be very beneficial.

I learned the value of work at a very young age. There is a popular saying that "work dignifies man." This is a great truth—only through work will you be able to find fulfillment.

HOW CAN I FIND SATISFACTION IN MY WORK?

This is a frequently asked question. But let's consider four answers that may help us in this regard.[1]

1. **Know Who You Are Working For**
   We are not just working for our client, our boss, or the owner of the company. Ultimately, we are working for the Lord. He is the boss of our boss. If we remember this every day, our attitude will change. In everything, we should work for the glory of God, "with all your heart, as working for the Lord, not for human masters" (Col 3:23). Your employer, your client, your family, the poor, and society as a whole deserve work that is done as unto the Lord.

2. **Make Your Work Benefit You**
   How is your job helping you grow as a Christian? Is your work contributing to this process? God does not want us to limit our service and worship to him only to church meetings. He wants to be involved in every aspect of our work. He cares about how we make sales, how we treat our boss, clients and colleagues, our employees, how we handle company property, daily irritations, and major crises that arise. He cares about how we represent him in our jobs, as Paul says that whatever we do should be for the glory of God (1 Cor 10:31).

---

1. DeHaan, *Find Satisfaction*, 8.

Times of stress and difficulties should be seen as opportunities to improve and trust God more, asking him for wisdom. Hardships produce perseverance, character, and hope. And even if we do not always receive the recognition or the salary we deserve, we can be sure that the Lord will reward the work done faithfully for his glory (Eph 6:5–8; Col 3:23–24).

3. **Keep Work in Its Proper Place**

   Work takes up a large portion of our time. If you work eight hours a day, that is a third of your day. If you sleep eight hours a day, half of your hours awake are spent working. Many people work even more than that. We can lose control of our work, allowing it to become our primary source of satisfaction, pushing aside family, friends, and church. For many, work can become an idol. The author of Ecclesiastes has already said that living this way is futile, as everything is vanity and chasing after the wind (Eccl 2:11). Life is more than a good job, a good salary, and a good retirement. Proverbs also says, "Do not wear yourself out to get rich; do not trust your own cleverness" (Prov 23:4). There is nothing wrong with being rich, but Solomon warns against pouring all of our energy into wealth while neglecting the other fundamental aspects of human happiness.

   We must maintain balance in life, and work is just one of its many important areas. We should neither overwork nor neglect work irresponsibly. It is necessary and a way to glorify God.

4. **Change Jobs or Not?**

   If you are unsure whether to change jobs or not, if you should seek something different that may bring more satisfaction, consider these four steps to discover God's will. These steps form the acronym P-A-T-H:

   a. **Pray about it.** Stay in constant fellowship with him, asking for the wisdom and direction needed to make the right decisions. Paul advises, "Pray without ceasing" (1 Thess 5:17 NASB).

b. **Acknowledge his principles.** What biblical principles apply to your decision? Will this decision be made with integrity, honor, and respect?

c. **Think through your options.** What are the available options? What are the pros and cons? How do your talents and abilities fit into this choice? How can you serve the Lord more effectively through this decision?

d. **Hear other people.** Talk to other people about your decision. Listen to opinions from those close to you and even from others who may have a different perspective. The word of God says, "For lack of guidance a nation falls, but victory is won through many advisers" (Prov 11:14). Others may see aspects of the situation that you are missing and can help you.

DO NOT AIM ONLY FOR SUCCESS

Albert Einstein reportedly said, "Try not to seek to be a person of success, but rather try to become a person of value." The success that the world promotes is based solely on having money, fame, and power. We have already discussed the importance of being practical—education and work to achieve financial stability. This is completely normal and desirable. However, both the Bible and history show us individuals who were well-educated and successful. Yet beyond mere success, they became people of great value. That is what will truly be your legacy—not just your possessions but the difference you make in people's lives.

The Bible gives us the example of Moses, who was educated in the finest institutions of his time in Egypt. All of this education greatly contributed to his calling—to lead the people of Israel out of slavery and into a land of freedom. His legacy was that of a prophet and leader who shaped his generation. More than just a well-educated man, his deep relationship and obedience to God set him apart in biblical history.

Daniel is another example of a young man who stood out. He and his friends were considered the wisest in their generation in that time. They dedicated themselves intensely to their studies, and God equipped them, placing Daniel in particular in positions of great influence and excellence. In the New Testament, we see Paul, who was educated at the feet of Gamaliel—one of the greatest teachers of his time. He used his knowledge for the kingdom of God and became a person of immense value, writing thirteen books of the New Testament. What is important is to use your knowledge, gifts, and resources to become a Christian of value.

Daniel Darling, in his book *Teen People of the Bible: Celebrity Profiles of Real Faith and Tragic Failure* tells the story of the famous American football player Danny Wuerffel. Despite all his fame and the lucrative opportunities he had as a coach or sports commentator, he chose to use his success to develop a ministry helping teenagers in inner-city New York, an area devastated by crime and poverty. Danny continues to dedicate his wealth, influence, and talents for the glory of God. More than just a successful person, Danny became a person of value.[2]

A SOURCE OF PROFIT

There is no perfect job where everything works smoothly. Frustrations and other challenges will always be part of the journey. However, it is possible to find contentment in what you do. Paul's words are deeply impactful: "Godliness with contentment is great gain" (1 Tim 6:6). What Paul is saying is that godliness (authentic spirituality) combined with contentment is like receiving a great salary.

Paul frequently used the word "godliness" in his letters to Timothy. For him, godliness always walked hand in hand with contentment. In Greek and Roman philosophy, this word often represented self-sufficiency—the ability to rely on one's own resources and not

---

2. Darling, *Teen People*, 30.

on others. For Stoic philosophers, the ideal person was someone who was completely independent, needing nothing and no one. However, Paul saw it differently. From a prison cell, he wrote to the Philippian Christians, "I can do all this through him who gives me strength" (Phil 4:13). He had faced countless life challenges, but through it all God had been with him. Now, he had learned to adapt to any situation. As Bible scholar Gary Inrig explains,

> This contentment is not self-sufficiency but Christ-sufficiency. It is not resignation—it is satisfaction. It is not merely accepting our social status or abandoning ambition, but submitting to Christ and His purposes. Godly contentment is neither complacency nor passivity, nor is it an unnatural detachment from life. Rather, as G. K. Chesterton said, "It is the ability to get everything that is in a situation." It is a deeply rooted perspective, a gift from Christ.[3]

We can—and should—apply our godliness and contentment to our work. Certainly, it will become a great source of profit.

FOR REFLECTION

1. How do you view your work as an opportunity to grow in all areas of your life?
2. Have you used your workplace as a mission field? If so, how?

A PRAYER

Lord, thank you for the job you have given me. I ask that you help me become a better professional each day and contribute to the growth and well-being of those around me. May your Holy Spirit use me in my workplace to be a witness of your love and to lead people to you. Amen.

3. Inrig, *Cultivating*, 13.

11

Waiting on the Lord

The best waiting is waiting on God! His answer comes at the right time and in the right way.[1]

Daniel Vieira da Silva

One of the hardest things for most of us is waiting. And since things don't always happen when we want them to, we struggle through the process. I remember a time in my life when I was eagerly waiting to be able to drive. I counted down the days until I could get my license and one day own a car.

The truth is, I have always been a bit restless, and waiting only made that more apparent. Whether it was waiting in line at the supermarket, waiting for my wife to get ready, or waiting for traffic to move, patience was never my strong suit. However, over the years, I have learned to be more patient—I've made progress, though I am still a work in progress. But I've realized that impatience isn't

---

1. Originally in Portuguese: *A melhor espera, é esperar em Deus! Dele a resposta vem certa e vem no tempo certo.*

just my problem. Why do we crave fast food, rely on microwaves, and consume quick online courses? Why are we drawn to short-form content like thirty-second reels and stories? Has time really sped up, or have we simply become more impatient?

WHAT DOES THE BIBLE SAY?

The Bible provides valuable lessons on time and waiting. Consider these passages:

> He has made everything beautiful in its time. He has also set eternity in the human heart; yet no one can fathom what God has done from beginning to end. (Eccl 3:11)

> God will bring into judgment both the righteous and the wicked, for there will be a time for every activity, a time to judge every deed. (Eccl 3:17)

> Teach us to number our days, that we may gain a heart of wisdom. (Ps 90:12)

> Be very careful, then, how you live—not as unwise but as wise, making the most of every opportunity, because the days are evil. (Eph 5:15-16)

ECCLESIASTES 3:1-8—UNDERSTANDING LIFE'S SEASONS

> To everything there is a season,
> A time for every purpose under heaven:
> A time to be born,
> And a time to die;
> A time to plant,
> And a time to pluck what is planted;
> A time to kill,
> And a time to heal;
> A time to break down,

And a time to build up;
A time to weep,
And a time to laugh;
A time to mourn,
And a time to dance;
A time to cast away stones,
And a time to gather stones;
A time to embrace,
And a time to refrain from embracing;
A time to gain,
And a time to lose;
A time to keep,
And a time to throw away;
A time to tear,
And a time to sew;
A time to keep silence,
And a time to speak;
A time to love,
And a time to hate;
A time of war,
And a time of peace. (NKJV)

UNDERSTANDING THE PASSAGE CORRECTLY

It is essential to interpret this passage correctly to avoid misunderstandings. The author of Ecclesiastes is not presenting a life formula but rather describing what life is instead of what it should be. These verses reflect reality, not moral instructions. For example, the text does not say that there is a time when we should kill, but rather that killing happens in the course of life. In the context of ancient Israel, there were instances where taking a life was permitted as a form of justice under the law of Moses.

Life has its seasons, but this does not mean we are bound by fatalism. Regarding this, Dr. Russell Shedd warns against a false theory that suggests:

> Each person's life is predetermined, and nothing can change its course. That human beings are mere actors

on the stage of life, unable to alter the roles they play. If this were true, then prayer would be meaningless, and God's warnings and instructions for life would have no significance. But Solomon does not support such a view.[2]

The key takeaway is that God created time, and different situations occur at different moments in our lives. Solomon continues by affirming that God has made everything beautiful in its time and has placed eternity in the human heart (Eccl 3:11). This means that we have an awareness that there is something beyond ourselves—something greater. For Christians, the apostle Paul expands on this idea when he writes, "And we know that all things work together for good to those who love God, to those who are called according to His purpose" (Rom 8:28 NKJV). This means that no matter the season we are in, God is sovereign, and everything is ultimately working toward his divine plan.

DIFFERENT TIMES

A powerful passage that highlights the difference between our timing and God's is Isa 55:8–9: "'For My thoughts are not your thoughts, Nor are your ways My ways,' says the Lord. 'For as the heavens are higher than the earth, So are My ways higher than your ways, And My thoughts than your thoughts.'" At first glance, this verse speaks of thoughts and ways, not time. However, God's thoughts and purposes unfold within time—his time, not ours.

We can say that God's time is higher than ours, meaning that his plans unfold at the right moment, often not when we expect. Paul affirms this in Gal 4:4—"But when the fullness of time had come, God sent forth His Son" (NASB). This phrase—*fullness of time*—refers to the precise and perfect moment determined by God to fulfill his will. Many Jews at the time, however, did not recognize this moment as the coming of the Messiah. They expected something different, and even today, some believe the *fullness of time* has yet to arrive.

---

2. SHEDD, *Bible Shedd*, 1590.

Similarly, we often fail to understand God's timing, which can lead to anxiety and frustration.

HOPING AGAINST HOPE—TRUSTING WHEN IT SEEMS IMPOSSIBLE

There are times in life when doubt begins to grow, and waiting feels like a burden too heavy to bear. These seasons often come when we hope for things to happen on our schedule, only to watch them unfold much later than we imagined. In those quiet, trying moments, God gently whispers, "Wait . . . just wait." Yet, our hearts resist the stillness, yearning for answers now.

Pastor and author Jaime Kemp offers a profound analogy about suffering and waiting: "In times of pain, God controls two crucial factors: The thermometer—how much heat is allowed. The clock—how long the heat will last."[3]

This truth is evident in the story of Abraham and Sarah. God promised them a son in their old age, and through that child a great nation would emerge, blessing all people on earth. God swore by himself that the promise would be fulfilled (Heb 6:13-15). Their only task was to trust him completely.

And time passed. Five years. Ten years. Fifteen years. Twenty years. And still—no child. By the time Abraham was one hundred years old and Sarah was ninety, God reaffirmed his promise (Gen 17:15-17). Abraham laughed. Can we blame him? It seemed impossible. Sarah also laughed, doubting in the face of prolonged waiting. Yet, when the promise was finally fulfilled, God named the child Isaac, which in Hebrew means "laughter." Despite their initial doubts, Paul tells us that Abraham ultimately believed: "Against all hope, Abraham in hope believed" (Rom 4:18) Jaime Kemp explains this phrase beautifully:

---

3. *No momento da dor Deus controla dois fatores importantes: o termômetro—quanto calor pode ser liberado—e o relógio—por quanto tempo o calor deve perdurar.* Kemp, *Gente como a gente*, 166.

What does it mean to "hope against hope"? It means believing when there is no logic, no reason, no probability. When all human analysis says it's impossible. When nature itself says "no." Have you ever heard of a 90-year-old woman conceiving and giving birth to a healthy child? Abraham's faith was the ultimate example of believing despite doubt. He trusted even when it seemed like God was silent. He trusted even when waiting took 25 years. He trusted in a sovereign, all-powerful God who can control and override the very laws of nature. This is the essence of faith in God's timing. It's not just waiting. It's trusting while we wait.[4]

WAITING WITH FAITH

Romans 4:20 tells us something incredible about Abraham's faith: "Yet he did not waver through unbelief regarding the promise of God, but was strengthened in his faith and gave glory to God" (Rom 4:20). Abraham glorified God while waiting—not after the promise was fulfilled, but during the long years of uncertainty. He trusted not in the circumstances, but in the character of God. This is a powerful lesson for us. When God gives us a promise, our response should be to praise him in the waiting. It wasn't easy for Abraham and Sarah to wait so many years, and it's not always easy for us either. But they chose to trust the one who is faithful.

---

4. *O que dizer "esperar contra a esperança"? Isso acontece quando não há lógica, não há bom senso, nenhuma probabilidade mediante a análise humana. Quando um corpo cessa inteiramente sua função de procriar, é impossível fazê-lo voltar a exercê-la (ao menos até hoje). Ou você já ouviu falar de alguma senhora de noventa anos que tenha engravidado e dado à luz um filho sadio e perfeito? Abraão, esperando contra a esperança, creu, para vir a ser pai de muitas nações, segundo lhe fora dito: Assim será a sua descendência.... Esta é a melhor ilustração bíblica a respeito da fé. Crer mesmo diante do ataque da dúvida. Crer mesmo quando Deus, aparentemente, diz não. Crer, mesmo durante o período de espera, quer ele seja de seis ou 25 anos. Crer em um Deus soberano e todo poderoso que é perfeitamente capaz de controlar e modificar as regras da natureza estipuladas por ele mesmo.* Kemp, *Gente como a gente,* 170.

The best thing we can do while waiting is to glorify God. Hebrews 6:13 gives us another incredible truth: "For when God made a promise to Abraham, since he had no one greater by whom to swear, he swore by himself" (ESV). This means that God's promises rest on his own name and character. Since he swore by himself, his very reputation is at stake. And God never fails to honor his name!

AN UNEXPECTED NEWS

I remember a time of waiting in my life that was deeply significant. What started as a simple act of donating blood for my grandfather turned into a moment that shook my world. During the routine testing, I was diagnosed with hepatitis C. Fear and uncertainty filled my heart. How did this happen? What would this mean for my future? No one in my family had dealt with this before, and we had no clear answers.

I started treatment immediately, taking daily medication and injections. The doctors made it clear—there were no guarantees of healing. If the medication didn't work, my liver could suffer severe consequences. But in those moments of fear, I clung to God. He is not just the God of the mountains but also of the valleys—even the valley of the shadow of death. This was a season of deep trials for me, but I knew God would intervene. A promise had been given, and many were praying on my behalf. I sought the Lord more than ever, pouring my heart out in his presence. I continued going to church, worshiping, and listening to his word. And then, one day, after a long period of treatment I took another round of tests. The results? Completely healed. To the glory of God!

WAITING IN THE VALLEY

The waiting period during trials can be overwhelming. Walking through the valley is anything but encouraging—it drains our strength and joy. But it is precisely in these moments that we must cling to the truth of God's word. David, a man familiar with hardships, declared: "Even though I walk through the darkest valley, I will fear no evil, for you are with me; your rod and your staff, they comfort me" (Ps 23:4). The *Full Life Study Bible* provides a powerful insight into this verse:

> In times of danger, difficulty, and even death, the believer does not fear any evil. Why? Because "You are with me" in all circumstances of life (cf. Matthew 28:20). The "rod" (a short wooden club) serves as a weapon for defense or discipline, symbolizing God's strength, power, and authority (cf. Exodus 21:20; Job 9:34). The "staff" (a long, slender stick with a hook at the end) is used to bring the sheep closer to the shepherd, guide them on the right path, or pull them away from danger. God's rod and staff assure us of His love and guidance in our lives (cf. Psalm 71:21; 86:17).[5]

David, who personally experienced years of waiting, understood what it meant to trust in God's timing. Though he was anointed as king in his youth, he had to wait twenty-two years before fully reigning over Israel. That's why his words in Ps 27:14 are so powerful: "Wait for the Lord; be strong and take heart and wait for the Lord." Notice the pattern: When we wait on our own, our strength fades over time. But when we wait on the Lord, he renews and strengthens our hearts! This is a divine paradox, what should weaken us actually makes us stronger when we wait in him. Glory to God!

WAITING PRODUCES GROWTH

Paul tells us that when we are in tribulation, in a time of waiting, certain things are produced in us. The first of these is patience. And who doesn't need an extra dose of this virtue? Patience produces experience. What a beautiful, serene, and respectable word. When we say that someone has experience in a particular area, we admire this quality with respect and credibility. In the language of sports, it is common to say that a team was very good with many

---

5. *Full Life Study Bible*, 833–34.

talented players but did not win because it lacked experience. In other words, talent alone was not enough; the team needed experienced players to lead them through in such a way as to win the game. Experience will be a great tutor in our lives, teaching us not only theoretically but also through real-life experiences.

And experience produces hope, and hope does not bring confusion (Rom 5:3–5). This is growth, maturity—a necessary work in us. Matthew Henry says,

> Tribulation produces patience, not in itself nor by itself, but through the powerful grace of God operating in and with tribulation. Those who suffer with patience receive abundant divine consolations when afflictions abound. It brings about a necessary experience for us.[6]

In a Spanish version of the Bible, *Nueva Reina Valera* (NRV), Rom 5:3-4 says, *La paciencia produce un carácter probado; y un carácter probado produce esperanza* ("Patience produces an approved character, and an approved character produces hope"). Certainly, God brings great transformations in us while we wait on him.

IN WAITING, WE GLORIFY GOD

We know that the purpose of God redeeming mankind is "for the praise of his glory" (Eph 1:6, 12, 14). All things were made by him, through him, and for him: "To Him be the glory forever! Amen" (Rom 11:36). Because of this, he himself tells us to "be still" (Ps 46:10), which in the original Hebrew (*raphah*) means "relax."

That is why we glory in our struggles, as Paul wrote to the Romans, because in this waiting—which produces many things in us—God is glorified. He says, "Not only so, but we also glory in our sufferings, because we know that suffering produces perseverance; perseverance, character; and character, hope. And hope does not put us to shame, because God's love has been poured out into our hearts through the Holy Spirit, who has been given to us" (Rom 5:3–5).

---

6. Henry, *Matthew Henry's Commentary*, 929.

The professor and writer J. I. Packer comments,

> Now we see that He leaves us in a world of sin to be tempted, tested, and broken by problems that threaten to crush us so that we may glorify Him through our patience in suffering, and so that He may show the riches of His grace and draw from us new praises, for He constantly sustains and delivers us. Psalm 107 is a majestic declaration of this truth.[7]

Is this a hard word to accept? Not for those who have come to understand that, in our waiting and patience, God is glorified. True faith finds its strength in honoring God through unwavering endurance, just as the psalmist declared, "Lord, I wait for you; you will answer, Lord my God." (Ps 38:15). It is the deep assurance that whether we walk through mountains or valleys, storms or struggles, the all-sufficient power of Christ rests upon us. It is the steadfast belief that God's way is not only best for our joy but ultimately for his glory.

A PROMISE

The messianic prophet Isaiah, in the fortieth chapter of his book, speaks about the deliverance promised to the people of Israel. This deliverance would not only be the defeat of their enemies at that time, but the ultimate victory would be in the future. The chapter begins by introducing John the Baptist, the "voice crying in the wilderness," preparing the way for the Messiah. Then the text says that the glory of the Lord will be revealed, his word endures forever, and the Lord will come with a mighty arm.

The text continues for several verses emphasizing God's wisdom, greatness, majesty, and creative power. All these descriptions inspire us to trust in this wonderful God. But at the end of the chapter, Israel still questions and is distressed by what they are going through. The prophet wonders, considering everything

---

7. Packer, *God's Plans for You*, 30–31.

described about the Lord, how Israel could say that God does not see them or care about their situation.

Perhaps you are having similar thoughts. Does God not see what I am going through? Isaiah responds, "Do you not know? Have you not heard? The Lord is the everlasting God, the Creator of the ends of the earth. He will not grow tired or weary, and his understanding no one can fathom" (v. 28). But we get tired. We grow weary of waiting and lose our strength many times. Then the prophet concludes, "But those who hope in the Lord will renew their strength. They will soar on wings like eagles; they will run and not grow weary, they will walk and not be faint" (v. 31). And this promise comforts us, for his word is true. We can wait on the Lord, and he will renew our strength.

FOR REFLECTION

1. How has your process of waiting for something from the Lord been?
2. What benefits have you experienced as a result of waiting on the Lord?

A PRAYER

My God, I trust and wait on you. You know what I have been asking and placing before you. I need your strength, and I ask that my faith be increased in this process. I know that you are working through your Holy Spirit in my inner being. I praise you for your action in my life. Amen!

12

Living the Word

The Scriptures were not given to increase our knowledge, but to change our lives.

—D. L. Moody

THE WORD OF GOD is not a book of information, but of formation. Our faith is not only based on an oral tradition passed down from generation to generation. We have a documented faith. And this written revelation of the holy Scriptures is not meant to be merely known, studied, or debated but above all, to be lived. That is why Paul emphasizes to the young worker Timothy that "All Scripture is inspired by God and is useful for teaching, for rebuking, for correcting, and for training in righteousness"(2 Tim 3:16 NASB).

LIVING FORGIVENESS

We know that fully living the word is costly, no matter how much we believe and teach it. I remember an experience where I was challenged to live out the issue of forgiveness, which is so strongly emphasized in the word. It was not just about a harsh or casual remark that can happen in human interactions, but rather an untruth spoken by someone that damaged my reputation. That hurt me deeply because I thought we had been friends for years, and I genuinely cared about this person and his family.

I was then challenged to live out what I consider one of the greatest characteristics of a Christian that is forgiveness. I confess that it was very difficult. I postponed it for some time, became indifferent, and distanced myself. However, forgiveness is not just about remaining silent and keeping your distance. Joseph could have forgiven his brothers and simply said, "You are forgiven. Safe travels." But no! Joseph forgave and invited his brothers to move to where he was so that he could take care of them. Similarly, the father of the prodigal son, who was deeply hurt by his son's actions, did not just forgive him when he returned repentant—he welcomed him back into the family. As the poet Ralph Waldo Emerson once said, "His heart was as large as the world, but there was no room in it to store the memory of what was wrong."[1]

And so I had to do the same—forgive. I did not defend myself, nor did I confront the person. And that decision was crucial for restoring the relationship. The Holy Spirit took care of removing all hurt and disappointment from my heart. Over time, their mistaken perception of me changed. Today, thanks to God, we are good friends again. Not long ago, I received an encouraging message from them along with an invitation to a barbecue at their house. Living the word may not be easy, but it is necessary.

LIVING THE HOPE OF ETERNITY

Hope is one of the greatest virtues of Christianity. No other belief or faith system compares to the hope that only a Christian possesses. It is the certainty that there is a beautiful place, prepared by the Father, waiting for us. It is to know that we are in the world,

---

1. AZ Quotes, "Ralph Waldo Emerson."

but not of this world. As the writer William MacDonald says, "For Christians, the world is an unhappy home but a good school. They are passing through the world until they reach their own country."[2]

This hope is not escapism or illusion. It is not simply accepting the world as it is, but also influencing it for the better. When we study history, we discover that the Christians who did the most for society were precisely those whose minds were set on eternity—starting with the apostles who brought the gospel to the known world, Christian scientists like Isaac Newton and Blaise Pascal who developed ideas that advanced society, and English Protestants who fought to end slavery. We could also name others like George Müller, who opened dozens of orphanages. If we truly long for heaven with all our hearts, we will surely have a greater impact here on earth.

The believer's hope is the certainty that all suffering will one day come to an end. There is a glory awaiting us. Paul expands on this, awakening the hope of the Roman believers when he says, "For I consider that the sufferings of this present time are not worth comparing with the glory that is to be revealed to us" (Rom 8:18 ESV). And to the church in Corinth, and to all of us, he adds, "Therefore we do not lose heart. Though outwardly we are wasting away, yet inwardly we are being renewed day by day. . . . So we fix our eyes not on what is seen, but on what is unseen. For what is seen is temporary, but what is unseen is eternal" (2 Cor 4:16, 18).

WAYS TO VIEW HOPE

In his book *Mere Christianity*, C. S. Lewis addresses the theme of "hope" in a very interesting way—in the unique style of this great theologian. He presents two incorrect ways and one correct way of viewing it.

The first wrong way is the *way of the fool*, who blames things. They spend their whole life thinking that if they just had something else, they would be happier. So they change jobs, spouses, homes, want more vacations, more travel. They place their hope

---

2. MacDonald, *World's Apart*, 23.

in the moment when they'll have all these things, believing then they'll be happy. But once they get what they wanted, they realize they need something more because they are still discontent.

The second incorrect way is that of the *disillusioned sensible person*. These are the ones who, at a certain age, conclude that it's all an illusion. They say that when you're younger, you chase happiness through accomplishments, but later you see it's not worth chasing the rainbow's end. So they settle for what they have and suppress the part of themselves that dreamed of something greater, choosing to accept life as it is. These people are, in fact, more mature and stable. However, what if the end of the rainbow *can* be reached? What if an eternal happiness *is* awaiting us? In that case, it would be a tragedy to discover, too late (the moment after death), that because of our so-called "common sense," we suffocated within ourselves the possibility of ever tasting that joy. The hope in this category has vanished.

The correct way is the *Christian way*. The true Christian believes that if none of the pleasures or experiences of this world can satisfy them, it is because they were made for another world.[3] Perhaps these "earthly pleasures were never meant to satisfy this desire, but only to arouse it and point us toward the real thing."[4] Therefore, we should not despise or be ungrateful for the blessings we receive here, but be aware that they are only a shadow, a foretaste of what God has for us at our final destination. And this hope must stay alive within me. I close this part by remembering the chorus of a hymn, which I translate into English: "Our hope is his coming, the king of kings comes to take us home; we still await you, Jesus, until the morning light appears."[5]

LIVING IN HOLINESS

If there is one aspect that most characterizes the Lord and distinguishes him from his creatures, it is holiness. It is no coincidence

---

3. Lewis, *Mere Christianity*, 134–37.
4. Lewis, *Mere Christianity*, 136.
5. Sobrinho, "Nossa Esperança."

that the seraphim the prophet Isaiah saw above God's throne were calling to one another: "Holy, Holy, Holy is the Lord of Hosts; the whole earth is full of His glory" (Isa 6:3 NKJV). It's interesting to note that they were not singing "powerful," "loving," or "good" (even though those are attributes of the Lord), but rather emphasized his very essence—holiness—which made the prophet tremble.

Because God is holy, he demands holiness from his chosen people, Israel. They were to be set apart, consecrated to the Lord, as expressed in Lev 19:2—"Speak to the entire assembly of Israel and say to them: 'Be holy because I, the Lord your God, am holy.'" But this requirement wasn't limited to his chosen people, because Jesus also prayed to the Father asking him to sanctify us when he said, "Sanctify them by the truth; your word is truth" (John 17:17).

Paul also urges all Christians, "Therefore, I urge you, brothers and sisters, in view of God's mercy, to offer your bodies as a living sacrifice, holy and pleasing to God—this is your true and proper worship" (Rom 12:1). And Peter adds, "But just as he who called you is holy, so be holy in all you do" (1 Pet 1:15).

THE NEED TO BE SANCTIFIED

Even though we know the biblical truths about holiness, we still fight a constant battle in this area, because if we are true Christians we know how necessary it is to pursue sanctification. The church urgently needs purification, but unfortunately, we see sin, dressed in many forms—large, small, or almost imperceptible, spreading and infiltrating the lives of many. God desires his church to be like a glorious bride awaiting her groom, Jesus Christ, for the wedding.

In his book *Returning to Holiness*, pastor and author Gregory R. Frizzell writes,

> I am convinced that the serious pursuit of holiness is in fact the very core of powerful prayer and of spiritual awakening for an entire nation. Unfortunately, in the program-filled (entertainment-driven) church, deep spiritual cleansing is either completely ignored or quickly and superficially mentioned. As a result, the people of

God are largely unaware of the subtle, unconfessed sins that extinguish Christ's power in their lives.[6]

It is these hidden, unconfessed sins that we must face in our lives. Chief among them is pride. As Saint Augustine wisely noted, "What is the origin of our evil but pride? For 'pride is the beginning of sin.'"[7] This sin—so serious it drove the devil from heaven—is truly dangerous. It often grows subtly, taking root in our strengths and achievements, quietly giving rise to vanity. Before we even recognize it, pride begins to take hold.

That's why in Scripture we see God condemning and punishing those who allowed themselves to be ruled by this sinful trait. Proverbs 16:5 says, "The Lord detests all the proud of heart. Be sure of this: They will not go unpunished." King Hezekiah took pride in all his treasure houses, silver, gold, and weapons, showing them off to a delegation from Babylon. Instead of testifying to them about the healing God had worked in his life, he boasted about material things. This displeased the Lord, who sent the prophet Isaiah with a sentence: Everything he had shown would be taken to Babylon, along with his descendants (2 Kgs 20:12–19).

To sanctify ourselves against pride, we must constantly examine our hearts and humble ourselves before the Lord's presence (Matt 23:12). The psalmist says, "A broken and contrite heart, O God, you will not despise" (Ps 51:17 ESV). And James adds, "God opposes the proud but gives grace to the humble" (James 4:6 ESV).

DAILY CONFESSION

If we want to live a full Christian life, we need to live a life of holiness through meticulous daily confession. This is not optional; it is absolutely essential. For God to move in our personal lives and in our churches, there must be deep repentance and purification among his people. This will lead to a revival whose central element is a return to holiness (2 Chr 7:14). Frizzell explains that "above

---

6. Frizzell, *Returning to Holiness*, 10.
7. Augustine, *City of God* 14.13 (NPNF[1] 2:273).

all, true holiness is not an abstract theological concept, but a person—Jesus. And if you allow Him, He will fill your heart with His glorious purity and His supernatural power."[8]

LIVING IN INTIMACY

Have you ever had someone in your life with whom you wanted a deeper relationship, but they simply didn't want the same? Maybe someone from school, work, or among your friends? The person is polite and courteous but distant! Sadly, some parents experience this with their children. They don't just want holidays together or gifts; they want connection! Or perhaps the opposite, children who desire that from their parents! No matter what you do, they just don't want to connect. It's strange—everyone is polite and well-mannered but still distant.

If we look through the entire Bible, from the Old Testament on, God is presented as someone who deeply desires more, yet the people stretch out their arms to politely resist. He is portrayed as the Father who wants a relationship with his son, but the son demands his inheritance to live life on his own terms (Luke 15). Jesus himself expressed this anguish: "Jerusalem, Jerusalem, you who kill the prophets and stone those sent to you, how often I have longed to gather your children together, as a hen gathers her chicks under her wings, and you were not willing!" (Matt 23:37).

BELIEVERS WITHOUT INTIMACY

In the book of Revelation, John writes a letter to the church in Laodicea, a wealthy city. God knew their deeds—that they were neither cold nor hot, and because they were lukewarm, the Lord would spit them out of his mouth (Rev 3:14–22). There are believers like that today—they take part in church activities, but because they feel comfortable in their lives, they think they can just "go by" spiritually.

---

8. Frizzell, *Returning to Holiness*, 12.

The Lord rebukes them because they didn't even realize the poor state they were in. And he says to those brothers and sisters in the church, "I'm here," at the door, knocking, waiting for someone to open so he can enter. It's as if he were saying, "You're good people, you have so many activities going on, ministries, celebrations, good works, events, courses—but 'I'm here,' outside the place where you gather, and I'm knocking!" You might ask, "How come, Lord? Just come in! It's your house, your people, come in!" But the word says, "If anyone . . . opens the door" (Rev 3:20). Throughout the entire Bible we see God seeking man—not in the sense of being unable to find him but longing for that deep relationship summed up in intimacy.

That's why many prefer religion. And religion becomes a substitute for what God truly wants for us because it is empty, mechanical, ritualistic. And Jesus said that religious people can reach a point where they are capable of doing terrible things because "they have not known the Father or me" (John 16:3).

HOW TO HAVE INTIMACY WITH GOD

Time. You need to spend time with him without rushing, without being in a hurry. Pray, read the Bible, meditate, be alone with the Lord. Today, many have replaced personal devotion with just attending church; worship with service; something personal with something institutional. And that's why there's no intimacy. Psalm 5:3 says, "In the morning, Lord, you hear my voice; in the morning I lay my requests before you and wait expectantly."

Transparency. We can't have a deep relationship by speaking in formulas. This means setting aside rehearsed or memorized prayers for a time! If we are angry, we shouldn't go to God saying, "Lord, I'm kind of upset." You're boiling with rage and you say "kind of upset"? We need to be sincere and honest about our feelings with God. The biblical characters never hid that. Look at the psalmists: "I am worn out from my groaning. All night long I flood my bed with weeping and drench my couch with tears. My eyes grow weak with sorrow" (Ps 6:6–7a).

Submission. This is often why we avoid intimacy with God and hide behind religion. Here's a profound truth: Submission is the most powerful relational force there is. When I offer my talent, my love, and all I do to God, the relationship grows deeper. Yet the very idea of submitting can be terrifying. We tend to keep our distance—close enough to feel connected but far enough to stay in control. We don't walk away from God entirely because we know we may still need him. But we stop short of full surrender. Why are we so afraid to submit? Because true submission means giving up control, and that goes against everything in our human nature. But that's exactly what God desires—that we trust him enough to let him lead, to hand over the reins of our lives.

WHEN THERE IS INTIMACY, GOD MANIFESTS HIMSELF

Because Daniel had intimacy with God, a miracle happened in the lions' den. The same thing happened in the home of Mary, Martha, and Lazarus. When the sisters sent a word to Jesus, they didn't focus on Lazarus's activism or work for the Master, but on the relationship between them: "The one you love" (John 11:3). Want to see the supernatural happen? Seek intimacy with the Lord.

That family's closeness with Jesus led them to experience a miracle. Not everyone Jesus healed or delivered had intimacy with him, but nearly every biblical character who *did* have intimacy with God experienced the supernatural in their lives.

When Peter was imprisoned, the church got on their knees. "The Early Church believed in the power of prayer—and God answered."[9] An angel entered that prison, set Peter free, and he was able to continue his ministry in the power of the Holy Spirit!

---

9. *A Igreja Primitiva acreditava no poder da oração e Deus atendeu.* Pesch, *Poder, cura e salvação,* 117.

ACCESSIBLE TO ALL

Many believers think that those biblical characters were a different kind of people—unlike us, mere mortal sinners of the twenty-first century. But the truth is, they were human just like us. Of the great prophet Elijah—who called fire down from heaven and was taken up without experiencing death, among other miraculous deeds—it is said that he "was a man with a nature like ours" (Jas 5:17 NASB). Moses, the meekest man on earth (Num 12:3), was once so enraged that he killed an Egyptian and smashed the tablets of the law written by the finger of God. Peter, the leader of the church Jesus established, was impulsive and unstable. In short, there are many flaws in the men and women of the Bible—yet they still believed in the Lord, and he used them powerfully because they sought intimacy with him.

They persevered in prayer, and so should we. As Charles Finney once said, "Every Christian possesses a measure of the Spirit of Christ—enough of the Holy Spirit to lead us into true consecration and to inspire us with the essential faith to prevail in prayer."[10]

I close by remembering the memorable hymn "Nearer, My God, to Thee" written in 1840, still incredibly relevant today due to its spiritual poetry. May the longing to be closer to the Lord lead us to live out the word and deepen our intimacy with the Holy Spirit until the great day of Jesus' return. Reflect on these lyrics.

NEARER, MY GOD, TO THEE

Nearer, my God, to Thee,
Nearer to Thee!
Even though it be through pain
That draws me near
Still all my prayer shall be
Nearer, my God, to Thee
Nearer, my God, to Thee
Nearer to Thee!

---

10. Finney, *Power from God*, 37.

Though like the wanderer
The sun gone down,
Darkness be over me,
My rest a stone.
Yet in my dreams I'd be
Nearer, my God, to Thee
Nearer, my God, to Thee
Nearer to Thee!

Then shall my soul sing
Thy praise, O Lord!
And raise in Bethel's light
A love-filled stone.
Still all my prayer shall be
Nearer, my God, to Thee
Nearer, my God, to Thee
Nearer to Thee!

And when, at last, my Lord
Calls me from here,
With seraphs in the skies
I'll dwell so near.
Then I'll rejoice and sing
Close to Thee, my King
Close to Thee, my King
My God, to Thee![11]

A PRAYER

Lord, my God, I want to live according to your word. I want to live out forgiveness, holiness, hope, and intimacy, just as the Scriptures teach me. Your word is the daily bread of my life and the light for my path. May I believe in the power of your word. Amen!

---

11. Adams, "Nearer, My God."

FINAL CONSIDERATIONS

Jesus said that he came into this world to bring us an abundant and purposeful life. At various times, we may even think this is impossible. But the life he speaks of is not free from suffering and challenges. Even the most devout Christian will go through them. The comfort we have is that the word of God assures us that he will be with us at all times (Matt 20:20).

This book invites you to reexamine key areas of daily life that significantly shape the abundant life Jesus intends for us. While many other aspects deserve attention, we've chosen to highlight these particular ones because, when approached with purpose, they can deeply enrich our spiritual walk. Life is intricate, and navigating it wisely demands both guidance and practice. That's why Christians turn to the word of God—it serves as a compass for every part of life. As evangelist Billy Graham once said, "The Bible is more modern than tomorrow morning's newspaper."[12] Even when we encounter modern challenges unfamiliar to biblical times, Scripture provides enduring truths that guide how we live, act, and respond.

The truth is, we've been greatly influenced by this world and by the evil system at work in it. We've distorted values, filled our time with trivial things, and our trust in God's promises has weakened. But if you, like me, sincerely desire to authentically live in Christ, we urgently need to reevaluate some aspects of our walk and change them. We must be doers of the word, not just hearers or readers. I am certain that the Lord is the one most interested in our continual transformation, and his Holy Spirit will help us in this process as he assists us in our weaknesses (Rom 8:26).

God deeply cares about everything we go through. He wants us to overcome all challenges through a life in Christ. We cannot leave him out of any area of our lives, as if to say, "This is spiritual, I need the word; and that is material, I need something else." We need the Lord's presence and his word at all times—whether in worship and fellowship at church, or even while browsing social

---

12. Billy Graham Library, "10 Quotes."

media. In everything, as Paul teaches us, whether eating, drinking, or doing anything else, we must glorify Jesus (1 Cor 10:31). Let us strive to grow, because Jesus desires that we live an abundant life, full of his presence and purpose. This is his promise, and we must take hold of it.

Bibliography

Adams, Sarah Flower. "Nearer, My God, to Thee." Hymnary.org, 1841. https://hymnary.org/text/nearer_my_god_to_thee_nearer_to_thee_een.
André, Christophe. *Imperfeitos, livres e felizes: Práticas de auto-estima* [Imperfect, free and happy: Practices of self-esteem]. Rio de Janeiro: BestSeller, 2007.
Artur, Pablo. *O fator Nazireu: A vida de Sansão* [The Nazirite factor: The life of Samson]. Londrina: Espaço Palavra, 2018.
Augustine. *The City of God*. Translated by Marcus Dods. In vol. 2 of *The Nicene and Post-Nicene Fathers*, Series 1. Edited by Philip Schaff. 1887. 14 vols. Repr., Peabody, MA: Hendrickson, 1999.
AZ Quotes. "Ralph Waldo Emerson." https://www.azquotes.com/quote/523247.
Banks, James. *Praying with the Bible*. Curitiba: Our Daily Bread Ministries, 2015.
Baptista, Douglas. *A igreja de Cristo e o império do mal: Como viver neste mundo dominado pelo espírito da Babilônia* [The church of Christ and the empire of evil—How to live in a world dominated by the spirit of Babylon]. Rio de Janeiro: CPAD, 2023.
Bauman, Zygmunt. *Liquid Love: On the Frailty of Human Bonds*. Rio de Janeiro: Jorge Zahar, 2004.
Bíblia de Estudo Pentecostal. Almeida Revista e Corrigida [Full Life Study Bible]. Rio de Janeiro: CPAD, 1995.
The Billy Graham Library. "10 Quotes from Billy Graham on the Bible." Blog from the Billy Graham Library, Feb. 10, 2022. https://billygrahamlibrary.org/blog-10-quotes-from-billy-graham-on-the-bible/.
Bonhoeffer, Dietrich. *Creation and Temptation: The Martyred Theologian's Lectures on the Biblical Pictures of Human Nature*. London: SCM, 1966.
Cabral, Elienai. *Integridade moral e espiritual: O legado do livro de Daniel para a igreja hoje* [Moral and spiritual integrity: The legacy of the Book of Daniel for today's church]. Rio de Janeiro: CPAD, 2014.
Crabb, Larry. *Inside Out: Real Change Is Possible if You're Willing to Start from the Inside Out*. Colorado Springs: Navpress, 1988.

BIBLIOGRAPHY

Darling, Daniel. *Teen People of the Bible: Celebrity Profiles of Real Faith and Tragic Failure.* Birmingham, AL: New Hope, 2007.
DeHaan, Martin R. *How Can I Find Satisfaction in My Work?* Grand Rapids, RBC, 2001.
Finney, Charles. *Power from God.* New Kensington, PA: Whitaker House, 1996.
Franklin, Regina. *In the Eyes of the Father—Our True Image in God's Mirror.* Grand Rapids: Discovery House, 2016.
Frizzell, Gregory R. *Return to Holiness.* Clermont, FL: Master Design, 2000.
Gonçalves, José. *Sabedoria de Deus para uma vida vitoriosa: A atualidade de Provérbios e Eclesiastes* [God's wisdom for a victorious life: The relevance of Proverbs and Ecclesiastes]. Rio de Janeiro: CPAD, 2013.
Graf, Jacob. *Falando francamente sobre juventude, casamento e família, à luz da Bíblia* [Speaking frankly about youth, marriage, family, in the light of the Bible]. São Paulo: Depósito de Literatura Cristã, 2002.
Guthrie, D., et al., eds. *The New Bible Commentary: Revised.* Grand Rapids: Eerdmans, 1970.
Henry, Matthew. *Matthew Henry's Commentary.* Grand Rapids: Zondervan, 2008.
Hummel, Charles E. *Tyranny of the Urgent.* Downers Grove, IL: InterVarsity, 1967.
Hurlbut, Jesse Lyman. *Hurlbut's Story of the Christian Church.* Philadelphia: John C. Winston, 1918.
Inrig, Gary. *Cultivating a Heart of Contentment.* Grand Rapids: RBC, 2007.
Jordan, Joe. *God, Did the Lord Call? What God's Call Means for Me.* Schroon Lake, NY: Word of Life Fellowship, 2007.
Kemp, Jaime. *Gente como a gente: Personagens bíblicos falam à família* [People like us: Biblical characters speak to the family]. São Paulo: Editora Sepal, 1998.
Lewis, C. S. *Mere Christianity.* San Francisco: HarperOne, 2009.
Lim, P. A. "Making Connections That Matter." *Asian Beacon* (2012) 8.
MacDonald, William. *World's Apart.* Port Colborne, ON: Gospel Folio, 2011.
McDowell, Josh. *The Bare Facts.* Chicago: Moody, 2011.
McLean Hospital. "Scrolling and Stress: The Impact of Social Media on Mental Health." https://www.mcleanhospital.org/essential/it-or-not-social-medias-affecting-your-mental-health.
Merriam-Webster.com. "Recognize." Sept. 23, 2025. https://www.merriam-webster.com/dictionary/recognize.
Ortlund, Anne. *Up with Worship: How to Quit Playing Church.* Glendale, CA: G/L, 1975.
Packer, J. I. *God's Plans for You.* Wheaton, IL: Crossway, 2001.
Pesch, Henrique. *Poder, Cura e Salvação: O Espírito Santo agindo na Igreja em Atos* [Power, healing and salvation: The Holy Spirit at work in Acts]. Rio de Janeiro: CPAD, 2019.
Provaca. "Juliano Spyer compartilha sua experiência no campo antropologia" [Juliano Spyer shares his experience in the field of anthropology]. YouTube, 1:29. https://www.youtube.com/watch?v=1jL1rbyij6I.

Bibliography

Shedd, Russell P. *Bíblia Shedd* [Shedd study Bible]. São Paulo: Vida Nova, 1997.
Smith, James Bryan. *The Good and Beautiful God*. Downers Grove, IL: InterVarsity, 2009.
Sobrinho, Almeida. "Nossa Esperança." In *Harpa Cristã* [The Christian Harp], 76. Rio de Janeiro: CPAD, 1995.
Stowell, Joseph M. *Living Close to God (When You're Not Feeling Very Spiritual)*. Grand Rapids: RBC, 2007.
Swindoll, Charles. *Strengthening Your Grip: Essentials in an Aimless World*. Waco, TX: Word, 1982.
———. *The Strong Family: Growing Wise in Family Life*. Portland, OR: Multnomah, 1991.
Thomas, Gary. *Sacred Marriage*. Grand Rapids: Zondervan, 2015.
Toler, Stan. *ReThink Your Life: A Remarkable Diet to Renew Your Mind*. Indianapolis: Wesleyan, 2008.
Warren, Neil Clark. *Finding the Love of Your Life*. New York: Pocket, 1994.
Wesley, John. "The Letters of John Wesley, 1739." Wesley Center Online. https://wesley.nnu.edu/john-wesley/the-letters-of-john-wesley/wesleys-letters-1739/#Four.
Witters, Dan. "U.S. Depression Rates Reach New Highs." Gallup, May 17, 2023. https://news.gallup.com/poll/505745/depression-rates-reach-new-highs.aspx.
Zodhiates, Spiros, and Warren Patrick Baker, eds. *Hebrew-Greek Key Word Study Bible*. New International Version. Chattanooga, TN: AMG, 1996.

www.ingramcontent.com/pod-product-compliance
Lightning Source LLC
Chambersburg PA
CBHW050837160426
43192CB00011B/2059